The Last of the Name

CHARLES McGLINCHEY

THE LAST OF THE NAME

❖

Edited with an Introduction by
BRIAN FRIEL

J.S. SANDERS & COMPANY

NASHVILLE

First published in 1986 by
The Blackstaff Press Limited, Belfast

First American edition published in 1999 by
J.S. Sanders & Company, Nashville

Text copyright © 1986 by Desmond Kavanagh
Introduction copyright © 1999 by Brian Friel

LIBRARY OF CONGRESS CATALOGING IN PUBLICATION DATA

McGlinchey, Charles, 1861–1954.
    The last of the name / Charles McGlinchey ; edited with an
introduction by Brian Friel. — 1st American ed.
        p.   cm.
    Originally published: Belfast : Blackstaff Press, 1986.
    ISBN 1–879941–45–7 (cloth : alk. paper)
    1. McGlinchey, Charles, 1861–1954. 2. Donegal
(Ireland : County) Biography. 3. Donegal (Ireland : County)
Social life and customs. I. Friel, Brian. II. Title.
CT868.M36A34   1999
941.69'3082'092—dc21
[B]   99–34726
                                                            CIP

J.S. Sanders & Company
Post Office Box 50331
Nashville, Tennessee 37205

Printed in the United States of America

1 3 5 7 9 10 8 6 4 2

CONTENTS

The Last of the Name

Introduction

THE LAST OF THE NAME IS A COLLECTION of stories and reminiscences of life in a very small parish in the northwest of County Donegal in the northwest of Ireland. The narrator is Charles Mc-Glinchey (1861–1954), a weaver; and the stories he tells of life in his parish have to do with the period of his own life and of the previous generation. He told these tales to his friend, Patrick Kavanagh, the local school-teacher who visited McGlinchey a couple of nights every week during the winters of the late 1940s and early 1950s. McGlinchey was then over eighty years of age and as he reminisced and wondered about life, Kavanagh wrote his words down because he knew that this was an acute and closely observed record of a kind of life that would never be seen again.

McGlinchey had very little schooling but spoke Irish and English and could read both. (On two uncharacteristic occasions in the memoir, probably to impress the transcribing school-master, he burst into bog Latin.) He never married. He outlived all his family and when he died in his ninety-fourth year he was buried in the family plot. "And after my day the grave will not be opened again, for I'm the last of the name."

The manuscript that Patrick Kavanagh's son, Desmond, gave to me to edit was frequently meandering and repetitive and one of the many rigours I imposed on it to give it its present shape was to break up McGlinchey's flowing, conversational speech into chapters and to give those chapters titles. (Imposing a literary shape on material that derives its character and vigour from a different form is an uncertain enterprise. It can be justified, I hope, if it makes that material available to a general public.) McGlinchey, reared on the stories of Fionn and Oisin and the Fianna—"stories so long that they wouldn't be finished at bedtime, so the old man would carry on the next night where he left off"—lives uneasily under that kind of regimentation; his remembering style resists such external structuring; a conversation has a right to be meandering and repetitive—maybe for emphasis, maybe for the music of the speech, maybe just because the old weaver is forgetful.

McGlinchey made only two short excursions out of the Meentiagh Glen where he lived his days. He went to Berwick-on-Tweed in Scotland one autumn and worked as a labourer there, "shearing and lifting corn and the wages were £1 a week with my keep." The second journey was to Dublin for the Eucharistic Congress in 1932. Neither expedition is discussed. Nothing but life in the Glen was important to him.

Meentiagh Glen is an important place, not in itself, but because an astute man observed it with love and his observations bestow an importance on it, elicited its importance from it. And that simultaneous bestowing and eliciting is the act of art. *The Last of the Name* is the work of an artist.

Brian Friel
Co. Donegal
1999

Chapter One

The Family

MY FATHER, NIALL, WAS A SMALL, low-set man but stout and well built. He was a weaver to trade and when he got a drop he used to say he was 'the best woolly weaver from Derry down'; and as far as I could hear, he wasn't saying a word of a lie. When any remarks would be passed about his height he would say, 'What about a couple of inches of skin and bone? If I haven't it in the length sure I have it in the breadth.' That's what people would say about a web of cloth.

I was born on the twenty-first of December 1861, in Meentiagh Glen in Clonmany. My father was born in the year of 1810, and that would leave my grandfather born about 1780. Some time before that the McGlincheys came from Glenfin away back in the bad times, and I heard of a well-to-do *bodach* of a man who lived there by the name of Peadar Ruadh, and he would be a close relation of my grandfather. The Scanlans were another breed that hailed from the Finn Valley.

Down to my young days there was nothing spoken in this parish at fair or chapel or gathering of any kind but Irish. A lot of the people in my father's time had some English and a few of them could read it. The English language came in greatly in my own time and in the one generation Irish went away like the snow off the ditches. But with the old people it was all Irish you would hear spoken.

My mother was Síle Harkin. She came from Urris, and finished up her life in the Glen and lived till she was ninety. She was born about the year 1824 for I often heard her saying that she was old enough to remember something of the *Tuilte Móra* [the Big Floods] that came in the winter of 1827. She remembered being up and through the house that night. These floods swept away all the bridges about the parish. The Meendoran bridge was built after the *Tuilte Móra* and lasted till the flood of 1945.

Her father, Seárlas, was born in the year of 1780. I was called after him. One night in the harvest-time of 1812 a boat crew were out fishing behind Dunaff. My grandfather and his two brothers and a lot more from Urris were in it. The wars of Napoleon were on at that time, and a ship of the English navy came close up to the Urris boat. Soon they saw a boat pulling out from the man-o'-war and drawing towards them. The crew fell to the oars then and were leaving them miles behind when the navy men opened fire on them, and sent a shot through the side of the boat, so they had to put up the oars and give in. They were taken then and pressed into service with the navy, all but a couple of *nachlats* [runts] of men that weren't worth taking, and they were allowed to take home the boat. My grandfather and two grand-uncles were taken, a relation of theirs, Donal O Dubhaigh, and whatever others happened to be in the crew. Anybody caught on the water [at] that time was pressed.

They were taken to Dublin and enrolled there and spent three years at sea in different parts, but their ship never took part in any of the fighting. They were treated well enough and got a pound of beef every day and a ration of rum.

Flogging was common on board ship in those days, and I'm told men were flogged to death many a time. There was one time Donal O Dubhaigh was to be flogged for something he did, but Donal always passed for a sort of a *cluasán* [blockhead, stupid person] and some of the headsmen let him off.

They got pay of some sort and a thing called result money, but they didn't get the result money till long after they came home. When the war was over, they were set free in Dublin and came home with £20 apiece of navy money with them. Shortly after that my grandfather got married.

One of the brothers that came home with him married a woman down in Clogherna that had a bit of land. There was a great run in times ago on women with land. He built a house for himself and bought a horse with the money he had home from the navy. The other brother got a woman with land, too, but he was dead before the result money was paid. He died young. The woman got the result money because she had not married again. The Waterloo priest, Fr O Donnell, came home from the war at the same time but he wasn't ordained till 1818.

My grandfather died in 1840 and was buried in the old graveyard in Straid. People could be buried there yet, as far as I know, for it's consecrated ground. That was the graveyard for the parish from the time of the Reformation, and continued to be, even when the old church was taken over by the Protestants, up till the new graveyard was opened in 1829. I always heard there was an old graveyard at Ard na Ronan in Binnion, and another in Bocharna, and one in the Glen in Drimaneich, on McDaid's farm, where they say a priest is buried.

When my grandfather died, my mother was sixteen and the oldest of the family. She was a medium-sized woman and a good carder and spinner. She did the cooking and the sewing and churning, and used to be carding or spinning, or cloving lint or heckling in the firelight at night. She was not a singer and I never heard her at any songs although she belonged to a *pór* [breed] there was music in. I heard her tell of an Urris woman who had her husband and two sons on the sea fishing. This woman had a rhyme or a prayer she used to say to the wind:

A ghaoith aneas chan le mo leas atá tú;
A ghaoith aniar chan de do iarraidh atá mé;
A ghaoith adtuaidh is gaol mo pháirt leat.
Tar anoir is tabhair na fir slán leat.

[*O south wind, you are not to my advantage;*
O west wind, I'm not asking you;

O north wind, I have a liking for you.
Come east and take the men safely home.]

When my mother would be sitting patching, I often heard a rhyme:

Is feárr paiste ná poll;
Is feárr loime ná lán;
Is feárr duine dona ná gan aon dhuine;
Is níl ann ach sin féin.

[*A patch is better than a hole;*
Thinness is better than stoutness;
A bad person is better than nobody;
And that's all that's to it.]

The old people had rhymes and sayings to fit different turns they would be doing about the house. At meal-time they used to say:

An dóigh is feárr ar do shláinte:
Coinnigh tú féin bearadach, brógach, brachánach.

[*The best remedy for good health:*
Keep yourself well dressed, well shod, and well fed.]

When my father was seventeen and learning the weaving trade, our present house was built. That was in the year of 1827, the year of the *Tuilte Móra.*

At the time of the Ordnance Survey in 1835, two of the sappers stopped in our house when they were mapping this part of the parish. My father went chaining with them whenever they would want him. They gave him some sketch of measuring land but he couldn't carry it out for he didn't know the rule of figures that was needed. The sappers were telling him their pay came to half-a-crown a day, and that was thought to be a great pay entirely, for working men at that time were paid 6d. a day, or 1od. for a day in the moss [bog].

One day the sappers were out on the face of Bulaba somewhere about Currachbeag, and they lay down to rest and take a smoke. When they went to look again, their whole kit was stolen, with papers and records of their work and instruments that were valued for £50 that could not be got nearer than Dublin. With the way of travelling that time, it would take three weeks to get them replaced. They came home and told my father. He questioned them if they had seen anyone about the place and they said they noticed a young fellow about the rocks before they sat down. From the description, my father knew it to be a fellow from that part who had a bad name. So my father went out to his home and asked him if he had noticed any men in Currachbeag that day and he said not. Then my father asked if he had seen a kit of tools belonging to them, and from the way he blushed he gave himself away, and my father knew he had him. So my father told him the sappers knew about him and were going to get a warrant for his arrest, but if the fellow handed the kit and papers over to him that he would stand between him and any other bother. The mother then told the lad who had taken them to give them up. So he took my father over to the rock where he had the lot hidden.

When my father came home with the kit, the sappers were delighted because they said the loss of the kit would likely cost them their jobs. They sent for a bottle of whiskey—that cost a shilling at the time—and they had a big drink. It took my father all his time to keep them from getting the young man arrested. He told them he had undertaken there would be no more bother and when they had got the kit to leave him to somebody else.

Just about that time, or maybe a year or two later, there was a Bible School going, and they were trying to set up Bible Centres in every parish. Youngs in Culdaff was the headquarters. William McLaughlin in the old rectory had a Centre in Dunree in the Buncrana parish, and my father got all of the books from him. They were in Irish, testaments and gospels and texts of different kinds.

One day the Rev. Molloy, the Protestant minister at the time, who lived in Dunally, called with my father. He had a lot of the Society books with him, and opened one of them and pointed out a chapter for my father to read. He read it without a stop. Then the minister clapped him on the shoulder and said he was the best reader of Irish he [had] met since he came to the parish, and if he took a hand to set up a Centre, the same as Master McLaughlin in the next parish, that he'd be under pay, and the pay would be advancing according as the Centre would be improving. Molloy could read and speak Irish well. My father refused.

The next Sunday when my father was at Mass, Fr James Doherty waylaid him at the chapel gate. 'I hear you had Molloy up,' said he. My father said he had and told him what happened. So Fr James told him to give the books back to McLaughlin and to have nothing more to do with them. Some days later we had the station [Mass in the home] and Fr James looked through the books my father had from McLaughlin. He put one of them in his pocket and said he'd deprive the Bible readers of that much. Fr James Doherty likely reported it to Dr Maginn, P.P. of Buncrana, for he called on McLaughlin and made him throw it up. McLaughlin must have been well in with the Society for he attended meetings in Culdaff every month.

That must have been before 1839 for Fr James Doherty was not in the parish at the time of the big wind that came in 1839. That was the stormiest night ever was in this parish, the night Robin Walker was born, I always heard. The Walkers lived in the Bridge House, the first two-storey house in the parish.

My father was at a school run by old William McLaughlin in the Glen before the time of the national schools. He learned to read English and picked up the Irish reading himself. I learned to read a bit of Irish myself the same way. My father always had a few Irish books of his own, mostly on religion, the Irish catechism and Dr Gallagher's sermons. He could read the sermons well. There was a great sermon on the Day of Judgement. The text was: *'Agus ins an am sin tifidh siad Mac an Duine ag teacht i néal le cumhacht agus caithréim* [And then they will see the Son of Man coming in a cloud with power and great glory].' The text in Latin was: *'Et tunc videbunt Filium Hominis venientem in nube cum postetate magna et majestate.'*

Dr Gallagher's sermons were great reading. No one going now will be saved according to these sermons, for there's nobody living up to them. I read the sermons myself many a time and I gave the loan of the book to Fr Mullan in Carn and never got it back.

Chapter Two

The Home

I NEVER REMEMBER ANY SOD HOUSES in my time. They were all built of stone and plastered with blue clay and lime. The people never bothered much about whitewashing. There wasn't much order on the houses then. The *cál leannógach* [algae, wall fungus] would be growing on the walls two or three feet up, nearly as far as the window-sill. The houses were roofed with bog fir and laths with *scraths* [sods] put on top of that with the clay side down. Then the houses were thatched with rushes or straw. The outhouses were often thatched with fine heather or bent from the shore. The thatch was tied down with home-made *súgáns* [straw ropes] attached to *bacáns* [hooks] stuck along the top of the walls below the eaves.

The chimney was just a rod-creel with no bottom. The smoke went up along the gable wall and out the hole, but a lot of the smoke hung about the rafters and there was a smell of smoke off everything about the house. Later on French hobs came in, and a flue was built to carry up the smoke. All the old houses had a couple of holes built in the wall at the side of the fireplace. They were called *poll-cloiche* or bowils. They would hold a pipe or fir-splits or things like that. There was always a kitchen bed in the old houses called an outshot and it was boarded off, with a sliding door to get in and out. It had a roof, too, and you could throw things up there out of the way. This was the taster bed. My mother said there were no windows in the house she was reared in herself, but two outshot beds, one to each side of the fireplace.

Her uncle took out one of the outshots and put in a window. But the roof was low, and his wife gave him no peace till he built a new house with a kitchen and two rooms. But people would tell you they had better luck in the old house.

In the older houses the bedroom was small, just the length of a bed. The wallsteads of an old house with a room of that kind are out in Gortnahinson yet. I stepped it myself and the room is seven feet long. The floors were either clay or flagged with flagstones from some quarry. Most houses had a half-door as well as the ordinary one. The door was fastened inside by a wooden bolt; and on the outside, if the people were going away for a day, it was locked with a padlock, a hasp and staple, that you got for a shilling. There was a latch, too, on most houses, a home-made wooden one or an iron one that you bought. The houses were hardly ever bolted at night, just left on the latch. A beggar could get a bed of straw beside the fire in nearly any house in the parish in those days.

The carpenters made the chairs and tables and dressers and wooden beds. People made three-legged stools, too, out of bog fir, and a house with children would have a supply of creepies or low stools that anybody could make. A lot of the old people never used chairs or stools but would sit on a bag at the fireside with their back to the hob or backstone. The Ogaster [Eoghan Roddy, a friend of McGlinchey] used to sit that way and always wore the back out of his weilycoat first. The weilycoat was a thing the people wore instead of a coat. It was like a waistcoat with sleeves and was made with long points in front that they could tie together. Some weilycoats had horn buttons. The weilycoat was made of white or grey or black wool and had no lining or collar. The trousers were white and grey and had a string tied below the knee. The knee garters kept the bottom of the trousers out of the wet and left the trousers full about the knees if a man was working.

In my father's time the height of fashion for men was a pair of black corduroy breeches buttoned at the knee with gilt buttons. The coat was a skirted coat. It was short in front like a waistcoat and had two long tails behind down to the back of the knees. The stockings were long and came up to the knee and the shoes were low but covered the ankle. All the young fellows at that time wore a castor hat. That was the whole style. Jackie McEleney and his brother Neil went to Carn one August fair day and got the sovereigns from their father to buy castors. The hats were that apiece. That's how they would dress up for the chapel or a wedding or anything like that. About home they made less do them.

My father hardly wore shoes or boots about the house in the summer-time. And it wasn't him alone but everybody else of his time. I knew a man in my time to get married in the second pair of shoes ever went on his feet. I wore no shoes myself when I was young. The men and women used to carry the shoes on their shoulder when going to the chapel until they got as far as Skeeog, and then they would put them on. They would take them off again on their way home. People wore *máirtíns* in my time. They were long stockings without any feet and reached from the knee to the ankle and the top of the foot and had a loop for linking over the big toe. The rest of the foot was bare. I wore *máirtíns* myself. All the women wore shawls long ago. They were not made at home but would be bought at fairs or in Derry. Bonnets and cloaks was another style with the women.

Up until my young days everything the people ate was produced at home. After the corn was threshed, every house got a *mealdar* [measure] of meal that lasted them for the year. In the morning for their breakfast people took oaten *brachán* [porridge] and milk or maybe oaten bread and milk. The oaten scones were hardened on an iron in front of the fire and there's nothing as tasty with a layer of butter on it as oaten bread. At dinner-time they took potatoes with salt and buttermilk, or maybe they would have herring or a bit of fish or a rabbit for 'kitchen' [anything outside the staple diet]. They used to call pepper and salt 'dab at the stool' for fun. Fish was a thing people went in greatly for. There was a Dr Kearney from Crossconnell, a son of Liam Bán, and he said if people used their own butter, and any money they put out on kitchen to spend it on fish, that they wouldn't need a doctor the longest day they lived. Dr Kearney used to bleed people from a vein in the arm. Bleeding is a thing that's done away with now entirely.

In the evening the people took oaten bread and milk again; and then a pot of *brachán* was made for the supper. For the supper, too, they used *sabhans*, made from the dust of the oaten meal. When it was boiled, it froze like carrageen moss and was very nourishing. People went to the strand, too, at the time of a *rabharta mór* [spring-tide] and gathered a *cnuasach* [load of shore food] of all kinds that made good kitchen—dulse [edible seaweed], *sliog* [shellfish] and carrageen.

As well as oaten bread they made flour bread, too, on the griddle. They made 'boxty bread' [potato bread] by grating down raw potatoes and mixing them with flour. Boxty is a thing I didn't see made for the supper. People, too, had eggs and butter, and hens and ducks and geese, and kept pigs, so they were never short. But nearly all the eggs and butter were kept for sale.

It was all wooden vessels they had at that time for there were no tins or pans or buckets. They had tubs and barrels and piggins [pint measures] and every house had a supply of noggins—*gugáns* they called them. A noggin held a quart. A long stave was left standing up on the noggin and on the piggin for a handle. The dishes were wooden and made all in a piece and of different sizes by the wheel-wright. The noggins and piggins were made by the cooper. Coopering was a great trade in times ago. There were six or seven in the parish alone. Now one cooper in Carn does all the work for the whole of Inishowen. The coopers put bulrushes between the staves and nothing would ever leak that the bulrushes were in. The Breslins used to cut bulrushes in the lough. Eoin O Breslin made a kind of a float with ladders and planks and boards and went out cutting the bulrushes with a long pole with a hook on the end of it. The rushes would be cut when in seed and tied in bundles and taken to Derry and sold to the coopers at 6d. a sheaf. It was a pleasant job on a nice warm day in August with your feet in the water.

The sacks they used before this were made of lint that was grown and spun and woven at home. They were very strong and gave great wear. Some of them held twenty-four stone and some forty stone. People had creels and baskets, too, the same as now. A thing that was in every house long ago was a *muirleog* [round, narrow-mouthed basket]. It was a round affair made of rods with a hole in the side of it. It was hung up on a peg in the side wall and held things like balls of wool or socks or *cruifleog* [odds and ends] of any kind. Cradles were made of rods, too, and had wooden rockers on them or sometimes were made to sit on the floor without any rockers or feet. The *muirleogs* are all done away with now.

At night-time there was no light about the house only what came from the fire. A woman or two used to sit to one side of the fire, cloving or carding or spinning with the light of the fire. The rest of the house would be in darkness. If anybody came into the house, someone always turned a turf in the fire to see who it was. The men sat about the kitchen chatting and telling stories or maybe singing sometimes. Some of the old people could keep the house going till bedtime. There was nothing else the men could do after night-fall.

I often heard my father telling about a night some men came to lift a woman from the Glen. Long ago women were often seized like that and taken away to marry some man. There was a mentioned girl named Betty Barr and one night a band of horsemen came for her. She had a sister, Katie, that wasn't so good looking. The men looked in the window and saw Betty cloving lint on a stool in the corner and Katie at the spinning wheel. The men moved in then but the girls happened to change places and they took Katie down the road where they had a horse with saddle and pillion ready for her. They discovered their mistake there and let her go. But they didn't get back for Betty for the Glen was alarmed by that time.

Seizing women that time was called *fuadach* [abduction/rape] by the old people. In my grandfather's time or before it there was a girl from the lower end of this parish seized and taken up about Kinnagoe or Buncrana. One Sunday afterwards her father saddled his horse and went up to see her. The people of the place were away at Mass about the hills somewhere and he found his daughter in the house. She warned him he would be in great danger if they came on him about the place. She made a scone for him called a *toirtín bog* [sponge cake] and hurried him away. They overtook him at the brook in the Glen that divides the two parishes. As soon as he got across and into his own parish, he turned to face them and put his trust in God and the *tearmann* [monastic sanctuary] of Clúan Máine [Clonmany] and fell to them with a cudgel of a stick he had and killed them as they came forward to him. The people that were killed were buried at that spot and it was always called Sruthán na gCorp [the Stream of the Corpses]. Many a time I fished that brook when I was a boy.

For going around the house the people used fir-splits. They were nearly as good as a box of matches or a candle. They made candles at home, too, with a lint thread or a peeled rush for a wick. This was dipped in tallow and let harden and then dipped again till it was thick enough. When they went to the byre to milk, someone took a coal and two or three fir-splits to show them light. If you were outside and looked about you after night, you wouldn't see a light far or near. On Christmas morning everyone lit a candle in the window and you could pick out the houses on both sides of the Glen when you would be going to early Mass.

At night the fire was always raked by covering the coals over with ashes. It was easy getting the fire lit in the mornings with good rakings. People rake the fires yet. I raked the fire myself one Saturday morning in 1932 and went to the Eucharistic Congress in Dublin and didn't get back till Monday evening. The fire was living in the rakings all the time.

People didn't make the candles at home in my time. They were to be got in the shops. Lots of the houses had small brass lamps without any globe. They burned paraffin oil that gave more light than a candle. Then the big oil lamps with globes came in, and sure now there's electric light and what-not.

In my early days there were very few clocks. People took their time from the sun. In odd houses you would see a wag-at-the-wall clock. It was always kept in the room. Men went round with packs selling and fixing clocks. A wag-at-the-wall cost £1. I remember a man by the name of Faller who went round the Glen when I was a young fellow. When he would be fixing a clock he used to mix up all the wheels on the table to frighten the women. They thought he'd never get them back in their right places again.

Chapter Three

The Land

HORSEBACK WAS THE ONLY WAY OF going a journey. There were few jaunting cars. They used to have a pillion on behind the saddle for a woman to ride pillion. She held on to the man's coat. At weddings it was common enough to see a score or maybe two score people on horseback. I heard my father saying the time Molshey Doherty got married they were galloping hard and beating races down the Glen road and one of the women fell off at Beanndubh and they never missed her till they reached Ardagh.

Molshey had a brother they called Charley Roe and he didn't know his own strength. They were ploughing one day and one of the horses took sick. So Charley loosed her out of the plough. He stepped in himself and got the tugs over his shoulders and pulled the plough till night-fall along with the other horse. He said it would be a poor man who couldn't take his turn alongside of a horse for a while of a day.

I remember when most of the farm work was done with spades and any ploughs going were wooden ones. They would be drawn by two horses like the one Charley Roe yoked into. The first iron plough from Meentiagh Lough to Meendoran Bridge was one Neddy Mc-Eleney got and the second belonged to Brian Roddy. On the same tack I remember the time there were upwards of fifty horses and now there aren't more than three.

The potatoes were set in ridges and kibbed, and all dug with the spade. The corn was all cut with the shearing hook. This hook had teeth like a saw but later on the sharp hook came in. A good shearer could cut twenty-five stook in the day. Hughie Gubbin was the best shearer I knew of. He could cut thirty stook at his ease. He worked with a man named Elkin in Termain. Elkin could cut twenty-five stook before dinner-time and then lay down in the sun till the evening and then he went round and stooked all he cut earlier in the day. Hughie said Elkin could give a pass to the rats. He'd write something on a bit of paper, and the first rat who got the paper would tell the others and they'd all head over the lane to the next farm and away from Elkins. Hughie was always telling wonderful things about rats and *whitterits* [stoats].

The corn was always threshed with the flail and then everyone made a *mealdar* of meal for the winter. There was a meal-mill and a scutch-mill in Cleagh at that time belonging to Leathan, and a lead to the Gortfad river kept them going. Both the mills were roofed with slates from McDaids' quarry in Ballintleve. Most of the slate houses about here long ago were roofed with slates from the same quarry.

There was little money in circulation in times gone by. People spent little and saved whatever they could make on crops or cattle or lint or butter. The run of wages was 6d. to 10d. a day. There was a boy hired in Termain at £4. It was the talk of the parish that anyone could earn such money as that. That was about the time I was born. Nobody was very much better off than another, except the landlords. They were on the top of the world.

Anybody that had a *cillín* [nest-egg] past them had it in gold and kept it about the house. I heard my father saying that when paper money came in first nobody had any belief in it. There was a man called Michael an Óir in my grandfather's time and he had a comfortable way on him and had money past him in gold. That was how he got his name. At that time there was a man in the Glen House by the name of Niall Seán Doherty and he got the loan of £100 in gold sovereigns from Michael. After some time he was paying him back but it was in paper money and devil a bit of Michael would take it back till he got it in gold the way he gave it to Niall Seán. And as far as I know he never got it from that day till this.

In my father's early days there was only one shop in the whole parish. It belonged to James Shiels and was the only house in the Cross at the time. The wallsteads are there yet. He was married to a daughter of Neal Roe Doherty. Shiels went to Derry once a week or so with an imitation of a cart with black wheels for whatever groceries would be wanted, soap or sugar, or salt or tea. Before that, up to about 1820 or so, the only commodities coming into the parish were iron and leather. Big Pádraig Doherty of Tirhoran and Andy Porter of Gaddy-duff (now Clonmany) and carters from Ballyliffin and Urris went to Derry regularly with cart loads of butter in butts and the only goods they had back was a supply of leather. It would be cut in soles and uppers and tied in bundles for different shoemakers that sent the orders with them.

Later on women went along with the carts to Derry and took back baskets of goods and went round selling the goods from house to house with their baskets on their arm. You could buy tea and sugar, or soap, or needles or pins from them. Anne Bhán MacCearáin went round the Glen and took one side going up and another side coming down. In my mother's time a man went round Urris buying eggs at 3d. a dozen. As he bought them he packed them in a creel and carried them on his back to James Sheils's shop at the Cross.

The roads at that time were only the name of roads. There was no order on them and they wouldn't bear a heavy load. There was little traffic on them except the Derry carts and they had thick wheels, half time with no iron shodding at all. People mostly took their corn and things in a sack thrown across a horse's back or else they used side-creels or a slipe-car with a big kesh creel on it. The slipe-car had no wheels but was pulled along on runners. The only fixing the roads got was a shovel of blue clay or gravel here and there where they would be giving way. In the summer-time there would be clouds of dust after horses or traffic of any kind. The seasons were better than now, and the weather was dead and warm in the summers long ago. The people used to call the last half of July and the first half of August the *Mí*

Mharbh [the Dead Month]. It was a time of great heat and flies and clegs. The cattle used to startle with the heat and flies, and stick their tails in the air and run before them all over the hill, a thing I didn't see happening for a long time till the summer of 1949.

In those days the roads in the winter-time would take a cart to the axle, for there was no regulation on them such as now. In my father's time Jimmy Butler was overseer for roads in these parts. He was the same Butlers as the Butlers of Grouse Hall and it was likely through their influence he got the job. Jimmy was married to a woman called Máire Muirgheasan. One day Máire was down along the road somewhere and she was attacked by a dunty cow, and nearly killed, till some Clonmany man was passing and drove the cow off. When Máire reached home and told all that happened the ones in the house said: '*Sé Dia féin a shábháil thú* ['Twas God Himself that saved you].' But Máire said: '*M'anam féin, nabh b'é ach gur fear as Clúan Máine é* [Indeed it wasn't but a Clonmany man].' The people in times ago were innocent.

Jimmy Butler had a big family. There was Rachel and Rebecca and Norton and Daniel. They likely took their names from the Grouse Hall people.

Another thing the carts took from Derry was iron for the blacksmiths. Blacksmithing was a great trade at that time. They shod the horses and made gates and hinges and crooks and tongs or whatever was needed. They made their own coal, too, for there was no coal brought into the parish till about the time I was born. They made a kind of coal out of turf. The turfs were heaped up, maybe three or four cart loads, in long low heaps and covered with sods or clay or *clábar*, the same as you'd cover a pit of potatoes. They were lit then and would smoulder away for a day and a night or maybe longer. But they had to be kept airtight or they would all burn to ashes. I remember my father going out at night to cover in one of the heaps where the blaze was breaking through. During the last war, when smiddy coal couldn't be got, there wasn't a man in the parish could make the coal from turf as they did a hundred years ago.

The wheelwright and saddler and cooper and weaver are other trades that are nearly a thing of the past.

In my grandfather's time, that would be about 1800 or thereabouts, people in the different parts of the parish used to take the cattle and pigs to the mountains for the summer months. It was only the women and children went, and Patrick's Day was the time for setting out. They built huts to live in called *bothógs* and the remains of these *bothógs* and some old pig houses can be seen about the hills yet. There is a place in Clofín bog called the *Bothógs* and it was there the people from that part took their cattle. William Grant's grandmother was born in one of these *bothógs* in Clofín. The pigs and cattle would graze through other. The women would milk the cows and make the butter. Some of them stored the butter in the soft moss and turf-men often came on a lump of it when cutting turf. I got a lump of five pounds myself and it melted into oil with the heat of the fire.

The men and growing lads stayed at home and worked at the crops, trenching a field for corn or lint, and making a ridge for potatoes. They used to trench a field and burn whatever was growing on it and sow corn. The ashes made great manure. At that time low-lying ground was soft and boggy for want of proper drains and the water seeped down and lodged there so that the people went in for working the higher ground nearer the hills. You'll often see marks of ground that was worked in times ago where the heather spead over again.

Butter-making was a great industry at that time and down till of late years. Cattle were better for milk long ago. The breeds they had suited the country better, though mad bulls and dunty cows were far more common long ago through sib-breeding. A springing heifer in my time fetched £5 or £6 but before that in the Famine times they were as low as 25s. with sheep at 4s.6d.

They would have six or seven pounds of butter to a churning, and the butter was packed in butts and salted. In Paddy Roddys I have seen butts of butter built up over the lip with a cloth tied over it. They would weigh over eight stone and would be two or three months gathering. The butter long ago was sold in the butter market in Derry, and later in Carn, and went from 4d. to 6d. a pound. No woman was considered fit for marrying if she wasn't a good butter-maker and a good spinner. They had pet names for the cows, Branney and Starry and Molly. When a woman would be milking she always called a cow *croidheag* [sweetheart]. '*Seas thart annsin, a chroidheag* [Stand around there, sweetheart],' she would say.

When the land was cut up about 1841 and 1842, everybody with a farm adjoining the mountain had a right of grazing over the mountain common. My father was entitled to graze over 114 acres, 2 roods and 20 square perches of the grazing in Bulaba and he had a stint of three *sooms*. A *soom* consisted of six sheep or three year-old stirks or one year-old heifer. As far as I know, all commons were stinted in *sooms* like that. I know Clogherna Green in Ballyliffin is stinted. Anybody putting on more than the right stint could be prevented, and if you hadn't stock, you could sell your stint to anybody else.

In my father's time and before it, people went in greatly for bleeding cattle in the summer-time. They boiled the blood with oaten meal and it was very nourishing. For drawing the blood they used a thing called a pair of flames. It had three blades with a spur at the back of each. The blades were of different sizes, the small one for young cattle and the others for older ones, two-year-olds or four-year-olds. They used to keep bullocks till they'd be five or six-year-old. A rope was tied round the animal's neck and a vein would swell till it would be as thick as a man's thumb. The spur was put on top of the vein and the man gave it a knock with a stick. The blood came out and was capped in a piggin. They took a quart or so of blood at a time. The two sides of the cut were then squeezed together and a pin pushed through and sweeled [wrapped] round with a thread. After a day or two the cut was healed and the pin was taken out. The old people said the stirk wouldn't start to thrive till it was bled. In the summer-time, when the cattle were all outliers in the hill, people had to sit up at night and watch or their cattle would be bled to death. My father was a good hand at bleeding cattle but it was done away with since my time.

Chapter Four

Poteen

THE REVENUE POLICE WERE APPOINTED after the wars of Napoleon. They were for putting down poteen. Poteen-making was a great industry at that time. It was all made from malt and malt-making was hard, troublesome work. The barley had to be steeped in a dam and then left near the fire and turned over till it all got warmed a bit. Then it was spread on the barn floor till it started to bud. As soon as the buds appeared, it was kiln-dried and grounded in a mill and steeped in barrels to ripen before it would be ready for running. There was no better drink than malt whiskey if the *fense* [dregs] was kept out of it. Lots of houses had malt-houses in times ago. The old house belonging to the Grants of Clochfin was the first stone house in these parts and was built about 1810. Under the room floor is a cellar for malt and you get into it by lifting a flat stone in the floor between the beds.

After the revenue police were appointed, the nearest barrack of them was in Derry and they used to make raids on horseback in different parts of the parish for poteen or stills. When the old people were afraid of raids they used to put a plank on the road with an iron rod sticking up on it and when they put their ear to the end of the rod they could hear the revenue men galloping their horses as far away as Buncrana nearly. When a still or worm or poteen was got any place, a fine was levied over the whole quarterland where the *úirlis* [instrument] was found.

With the fines and all, people took to making poteen away in the hills. Glashedy Island was another great hide even down to my own day.

One time the men came in from the island with a run of poteen and the revenue men came on them and seized the whole lot. But some men about Mullagh, who spent a while in the navy, heard about the seizure and came down through Mullaghreagh and attacked the police and took every drop from them again. The men were well armed with sticks and the revenue men were afraid of them.

All the old poteen-makers threw the first glass away. They said it was for the fairies and if they kept them on their land they would warn them some way if the revenue men were coming. The revenue men were for nothing else but for putting down poteen.

Later on there was a big barrack of revenue men in Gaddyduff. There were thirty-five men and a sergeant at one time. The inside walls of the old barrack were built of turf. After a seizure of poteen an officer came down from Buncrana to see that all the whiskey was spilled down a grating. But the men had a tub under the grating and before the officer was out of sight they were all enjoying themselves and had in some of the neighbours they were great with.

Before the time of the revenue police the country was patrolled by soldiers known as the Light Horse. I think there was a regiment of them about Carn or Malin. They used to come out about Pollan Green to catch poachers, for rabbits and game of all kinds belonged to the landlord. They chased Séamus Aindrias one night to the top of Binnion Hill but he hid on them behind Beann na Madadh [the Dogs' Cliff].

Another time the redcoats made a raid for poteen on Morrisons in Straid. There was a big party going on, and when the alarm got up, all the men went outside and left the women inside to hide the whiskey. The soldiers ordered the women to open the door, but they refused, and the soldiers put their bayonets through the door. But as the blades came through, the women broke them off with an iron bar that they had. At the heel of the hunt, the officer in charge—he was the name of Dalziel—climbed up the roof and started going down the chimney. The men outside called to the women in Irish: '*Cáith cochan na leabtha 'sa tine* [Throw the bedstraw in the fire].' So the women put two or three armfuls on the fire and smoked Dalziel out of the chimney and burned the clothes off his back.

It was long after that that the ordinary police were established. They were called Peace Men and were for keeping down fights between people and rows and disorder of any kind. The revenue men were all Protestants, and so were the Peace Men in the beginning.

I don't remember much poteen made from malt. It was mostly made from sugar and treacle in any time. Three or four stone of sugar would make three gallons of good whiskey, and half-a-gallon of *fense*. Many a time I made a run myself. A glass of good poteen punched was a great remedy in times of sickness.

Chapter Five

Spinning and Weaving

UP TILL MY EARLY DAYS LINT WAS the whole industry in this parish. It was dying out in my time but about 1830 it was in full swing. Lint and butter were the two ways people had for making a shilling. I remember the time myself when nearly everyone in the parish had a barrel of lint sown. I always heard the land that grew lint one year would grow as good a crop of corn the following year as it would after a crop you had to manure, like potatoes or cabbage. After being steeped in a dam the lint was scutched with a stick over a block for the purpose. Later there were scutch-mills. There was one in Cleagh and one in Cock Hill and one in Donagh. I don't think there's a scutch-mill in Inishowen at the present time. Long ago every house was hung round with bundles of lint scutched or spun in thread.

Women took bundles of lint for sale to Derry in my father's time. I heard of a woman from Tirhoran who set out one morning for Derry with her bundle of lint. It would be scutched, not spun. She drove the cow over the hill for grazing and left her there. She walked the thirty miles to Derry and sold her lint at 3d. a pound and bought whatever novelties she wanted. On her way back over the hill she took the cow home with her and had her milked before night-fall.

Micheál Seán Gráinne's mother started for Derry early one morning in August with her bundle of lint, and carried home on her back a four-stone poke of meal, and was home before the sun went down, and had a creel of weeds pulled for her cow at milking-time that night. Derry was the whole market for lint at that time. I heard tell of Katie McEleney and some other women from Glen being in Derry one time

with lint. On their way home, up about Inch or somewhere, they fell
in with a man going about turf, and he gave them a lift on his cart. But
Katie soon noticed it was a bullock he had yoked in the cart instead of
a hoarse. So Katie and the others couldn't be bound or held till they
got out and walked. They never saw a bullock yoked in a cart before
and got frightened.

It was a common thing to walk to Derry in times ago and people
thought nothing of it. I heard of a Clonmany woman heading for
Derry up over Pinch one morning and she fell in with a *banvil* [group]
of men cutting turf about Lagsalach. She told them her errand was to
get a pair of wool shears. One of them said he'd lend her a pair, but she
said when she was that far she'd go on. She was a mile from home that
time and had the best part of thirty in front of her. She was back with
the shears before the men stopped cutting that evening. But all the
women weren't as far travelled. Some of them never left the townland
they were reared in unless to go to chapel. There was a woman from
Altahall one time and she got to the top of Pinch. She saw the Swilly
and the hills of Fanad beyond. She says, 'Who would think the world
was so big? And there's America lying over there, you that broke many
a mother's heart.'

In my own time women took the lint to Carn and it went about 6d.
a pound. They went on the bare feet, and carried the shoes on their
shoulder, and put them on when they got as far as Churchtown.

If the lint was to be spun at home, it had to be heckled after it was
scutched. It was pulled across a board with nails sticking up in it.
Then it was cloved on a cloving stick. The cloving stick had a blade up
along the side of it and the lint was drawn through between the stick
and the blade. It was ready for spinning then. The same spinning
wheel did for lint and wool. The thread was put on the reel, and tied
in cuts, four cuts made a slipping, twelve slippings made a spangle. A
hank was a quarter spangle or three slippings.

The people long ago had gatherings for a night's scutching or
cloving of lint. There would be twenty or thirty at a gathering. They

did the work in the barn or some outhouse, and other times in the
kitchen. They had a dance after the work was done. Someone would
be got to play the fiddle, or two or three of the women would lilt. They
had gatherings, too, for making quilts. It was all women came to the
quiltings. They had a wooden frame to spread the quilt on which
they'd be working.

Any of the lint thread that wasn't needed for weaving could be sold
in the market. Some took it to Derry and some to Carn and some to
the fair of Ballyliffin. They would get 2s.6d. a spangle but that price
went up and down. At that time a gauger attended the market and he
could take a slipping out of any that was for sale, and measure it on a
stick he had. This was a measuring rod and if the slipping didn't reach
up to a notch that was on the stick, that bundle would be seized. That
meant the reel had been shortened and wasn't giving the right length
of thread. But if the owner knew the law, she could make the gauger
measure one cut, and if it measured up to the notch, the bundle would
pass. Buyers came to the markets but many a man in Ballyliffin and
Carn bought on speculation of the price going up.

A granduncle of mine, the one that got married to the woman in
Clogherna after he came from the navy, bought up a handling of lint
yarn one time. But instead of the price rising, a slack came on and he
could get no sale for it, and the whole lot went to loss on his hands. I
heard my mother saying he lost up to £30 at that time.

The weaving was done on the loom. Any carpenter at that time
could make a loom or repair one that got worn or broken. My father
worked a lot at weaving linen. It was used for sheeting and men's
shirts, for ticking and for towels and sacks. The weavers made a cloth
called *drogat* [*drogóid*—half-wool, half-linen] with a linen warp and a
woollen weft. It was mostly used for women's clothes. All the young
girls would have skirts and frocks made of *drogat* with the yarn dyed
red and blue. I started to weave myself at sixteen years. I was paid 6d.
or 4d. a yard according to the breadth, and 9d. for weaving *drogat*
because it was harder to do. The yarn was dyed at home after it was

spun. Logwood or indigo was used. There was always a pot of indigo kept warm beside the fire in every house at that time. Another great dye was the *crotal* [lichen] that grows on rocks. It gave a red or orange colour and was greatly used for dyeing wool. Later on the lint for ticking was sent to the dysters about Derry. The ticking would come out white and blue in the weaving. Linen weaving was mostly done away with in my time. Linen yarn was only used in making *drogat*.

The sewing was all done by hand, and it was lint thread the tailors used. Jeremy MacCarron was a tailor in my time. He used to go round and make suits and clothes of any kind in the customers' houses and took all his tacklings with him. He got his keep but would go home at night if he was working near. He got five shillings for making a suit. He always used homemade linen thread.

The old people had all a supply of linen sheets that would last a lifetime. My mother's people had sheets and sacks made of linen that wore for two generations. I heard that the O Donnells of Drumfries had a lot of the old linen sheets still of late, and they were lent out all round the country to dress up a death-bed. But doing up a death-bed in white sheets is nearly a thing of the past.

Some people used lint for thatching long ago, and it would last a long time. James O Donnell and John Carey of Drumfries were up about Beart one time for straw. The farmhouse they called in was thatched with lint that was black and green with age and James was thinking there would be some drops with a roof like that. They asked the farmer how long it was since the place was thatched, and he reached up and pulled down a few stalks of the lint and it was as good as the first day it went on. He said his father came to the place sixty-four years before that and he never remembered the house to be thatched in his time, and he thought it would be as long again before a new roof would be needed, and he never knew a drop to come through in all that time.

People made all the clothes they needed from the wool of their own sheep. I remember when there was nothing going into the chapel on

Sundays but home-made cloth. At that time the sheep were all Irish, and the wool was much finer than all the wool that's going now for it's nearly all Scotch or cross-bred sheep that are in the parish at the present time. When the sheep were clipped in the summer, the women scoured the wool by washing it in a brook without soap. It was then carded and spun. They dyed the wool whatever colour they wanted before it was carded. The women in every house used to sit alongside the fire carding and spinning till bedtime. The woollen yarn was never sold. It was all used in home weaving, blue suiting cloth, or white *báinin* [homespun flannel], or blanket cloth.

The best spinner I heard of was Annara Dhiarmada of Effishmore. She was my father's time. She used to card and spin a lot during the night when the house was quiet and would work on till the small hours many a night. One Saturday night there was a priest staying with her who was on his banishment. He was on one side of the fire and Annara on the other side, spinning. She had some hens clocking at the side of the kitchen. Sometime in the middle of the night a rooster jumped up on a creel in the middle of the floor and started to crow. The priest said to Annara if she'd take his advice she'd stop working after twelve o'clock on a Saturday night any more. A rooster crowing at any time during the night was a sort of a sign and people never liked it.

In Paddy Mór Roddy's house there was a roost for the hens down at the door, and one night at bedtime the rooster began crowing and flapping his wings till he frightened them. The old man was lying in the kitchen bed, and he asked the young people what direction was the rooster facing. They told him he was facing in his direction. Then he told them to feel the rooster's feet, were they cold or warm. They told him they were warm, so Paddy said the thing would go past without a death. That same night a son of Paddy's nearly died with a colic but he pulled out of it next day and got all right.

My father was weaving a web of cloth for Annara one time and he sent her word he'd need a couple of hanks to finish the web. Annara's brother, Neall, took a grey wether in from the side of Bulaba next morning and clipped him, and the women spun the yarn and took it to my father and had the web home with them that night. The old people used to tell of a man who clipped the sheep in the morning and had the suit made with the tailor that same night for a wedding he was going to.

I learned the weaving trade from my father and it came naturally to my hand. Many a night I spent at the loom and many a half-crown I made when other young fellows of my age were away at dances or ceilidhing. I could make a yard of blanket cloth in the hour, and that was the wide breadth. *Drogat* gave more bother in the weaving. The women gave me the yarn to weave in hanks, and I set it up in the loom. There were four treadle feet in the loom to get the different patterns. I could weave herring-bone patterns, or dice patterns, some with eight threads to the dice and some with sixteen. Phil Devlin of Ballinabo was a good weaver and so was Michael Harkin, Micheál Figheadóir [Michael the Weaver] he was called. Phil was supposed to weave a hare and a hound into a web of cloth, but that couldn't be done on the looms we worked with.

The shuttle was made of apple-wood or holly, and had two wire runners on the bottom to make it run over the threads. The reed was made of cane wood and had to be made by a reed-maker. There was a good reed-maker in Donagh by the name of Doherty. A reed cost 7s.6d. They were of different closenesses. For wool they had fourteen splits to the beer, and for linen or ticking maybe twenty-two or twenty-five a beer. That was the finest I ever used but you could get ones finer than that. At a lint cloving or gathering like that, some people could take right music out of a reed by putting a piece of paper on it and blowing on the paper. Children do it yet with a coarse comb. As a piece would be woven, I rolled it up on a beam. A weaver always kept a pot or vessel like that with water in it for wetting the work. That kept the yarn from breaking. But the yarn would break many a time and had to be tied with a weaver's knot. No other knot would pass through the reed.

If the cloth was woven fancy for men's wear, it was taken to the cloth-mill to be thickened and dressed and pressed. The cloth was put into troughs and soft soap was spread over it. Then it was dried and pressed. The blue cloth would be rubbed with a stiff brush and then gone over with a pair of scissors and clipped.

I didn't do any weaving this long and many a year. The loom went to wreck on me. I don't think there's a loom in the whole of Inishowen at the present day.

Chapter Six

Emigration

IN MY FATHER'S TIME ANY MAN OR young fellow who hadn't much to do at home in the summer went to the harvest in England or Scotland to the shearing. My father never left home. He had his trade as a weaver and had plenty to do at home. When he would hear of the good wages, up to maybe a pound a week, that were to be made across the water, he always quoted a saying the old people had: '*Chá mbíonn mil ar fheochadáin, ná ór ar dhreasóga i dtíortha eile ach oiread is atá sa bhaile* [There's no honey on thistles, nor gold on briars, in any other countries any more than at home].'

The shearing in his time was done with a toothed hook, and men going to Scotland often took their own hooks with them, hooks that they were used working with. They were paid by the acre. The pay was 15s. an acre, with their keep. They slept in the barn on a bed of straw, with a blanket over them. They were out in the morning early on a fasting stomach, and got oaten porridge and milk taken out to them at breakfast-time. For their dinner they got a bottle of beer and a shearer's loaf, no butter, not even a knife. They just broke off pieces and ate it that way. They had porridge and milk again in the evening, and that was the day's feeding. But they could do a great day's work all the same. Now it takes all the men of the parish two or three starts of an afternoon to cut the grass in the graveyards, what one good shearer could do in a day or two before this.

Before they earned the 15s., the corn had to be tied and stooked. Every man would have the bulk of £5 or maybe £10 home with him after the harvest, and that would come in handy for the rent that had to be paid in October, and the cuts [rates] due at holiday. The rents ranged from £6 to £10 or so, and the cuts were about half of that. It took a lot of gathering at the prices things were going, and wages 9d. a day.

The boat fare to Scotland was 4s., but when the *Dugdale* was running, they cut the prices, and I heard Paddy Mór McEleney saying that he got over and back on the *Dugdale* for 6d. a time, and got a bottle of porter into the bargain.

After the wars were over in 1815, lots of ones went off to America. It was all sailing vessels at that time. One of the Grants of Clochfin went to America and it took him three months. On the way over he got so seasick that the crew were for throwing him overboard because he was about dead. They had a sheet of canvas spread out to roll him up in, but some Malin men interfered and wouldn't let them throw him overboard as long as there was life in him. He lasted out the voyage and reached Philadelphia. Instead of taking work he got a pack and soon made the price of a house, and before he died he had a street of houses, and left all to a daughter of his by the name of Gormley.

At that time it cost a shilling to send a letter to America. That was before there was any post-office here. The letter had to be left in a house in Derry and would be sent on some ship to Boston or wherever it was going. It would lie there till the person it was for came to lift it. I remember myself the time the post-office was in Straid, when the people had to go there for their letters. There was no delivery like there is now.

I heard, too, of a man called Owen McCreevan who went to America in the old days, but with the storms and contrary winds didn't it take him half a year to make the journey. Nearly all their provision was used up. Owen had a good store of tobacco with him, and the captain gave him a gold sovereign for a small bit he had left. The captain's supply must have run short.

It was a common thing for ships to be lost at sea. They were wooden ships with sails and couldn't stand up to the storm. In my grandfather's time, in 1811, the year before he was pressed into the navy, there was a ship sunk off Dunaff Head. Big Tomás Carey of Owenbwee remembered the night well, when wind shifted round and drove the ship on the rocks. She sank a short distance from the shore, and the masts could be seen at low water for long after. The ship was called the *Saldannah*, and there was a song made about her. People say if she had kept out in the depths she would have stood a better chance. But the captain said he'd make Lough Swilly or Hell of it before the morning. In Desertegney that night a strange woman came into a house and sat by the fire and spoke to nobody. About midnight she jumped up and shouted: 'The *Saldannah*'s down.' She made out the door and was never seen again.

The morning after the ship was lost a parrot was found in the trees about Fahan, one that must have come off the *Saldannah*. All the parrot could say was: 'Poor *Saldannah*, poor *Saldannah*.'

A neighbour of ours, Paddy Mór Harkin, had seven sons, and they all went abroad in their time, except one who stayed in the home place. In 1841 when the land was first cut up, Paddy Mór lost the good bit of ground he had and his father before him. They were given a bare bit of heathery ground and lived under a rock till they got a sod house built for themselves. The bailiffs got their pick of the good land; and in those days, if you met a bailiff and didn't touch your cap, you'd find yourself out of your farm or maybe in jail. That year the Harkins had to get a ridge for potatoes in Gortfad and one in Carrohill till they got some of the heather broken in. One of Paddy's sons, John, was so angry that he packed up and went to Scotland, but died in a hospital there soon after. As the sons grew up they went to America.

Charley was the seventh son. The old people would tell you there was a cure for the 'evil' on a seventh son. Charley never worked at the curing, but Eoin O Breslin used to call him the Doctor and he wasn't half pleased about it. He was a fine strapping fellow. He could stand on the door-step at thatching time and throw a *ceirtlín* [clew] of home-made straw ropes over the roof without touching the thatch. It would weigh three stone good or maybe more. He spent a lot of his time out with the dogs and gun and had seven foxes' skins in the house at the one time. One day when he was footing turf on the bank, he took a cramp and was only able to make home of it. They got a doctor from Derry and he tried leeches to his side, but they did him no good. Then he said there was medicine in Derry that would cure him, but he would need to get it inside four hours. So a friend of Charley's, Johnny McDaid, saddled his horse on the street at ten o'clock. It was a moonlit night in June. He galloped the twenty-five miles to Derry and back again and jumped off his horse on the street as the clock in the room was striking two. The horse was in a layer of sweat and they turned him down the garden. He lay down and stretched his legs and head from him and lay that way till sundown the next evening. Then he got up and shook himself and started to nibble the grass.

The medicine did Charley no good and he died two days after. His two dogs hung about the house and would go with nobody else. Both of them were dead in a fortnight's time.

They paid the doctor £5. He was a Dr White.

Mickey and Denis, two other sons of Paddy Mór's, went to England for a year or two and then went to America. It took Mickey three weeks and three days one time going to the English harvest. He got work on a farm there and next morning the man of the house took out a pot of porridge to the field for the breakfast. There was a hole in the porridge for each man, with milk and a spoon in it. Mickey stood with his back to a tree, so the boss came back and asked why he wasn't eating. Mickey said he wanted his food right, that he wasn't reared that way. So he was taken inside and got his meals at the table from that on.

Mickey always wore a white ball hat made of a sort of rubber or gutta-percha. They were called ball hats. Next year his brother Denis went over to the same farmhouse, and when the farmer got his name he called to his wife: 'Here's a brother of White Hat's. He'll have to get his meals in the house.'

Denis went to America about the year of 1850. It took the ship seven weeks and three days to cross over. The sailing vessels would have to take down sails if a storm got up, and they would often be blown back in one day what they went forward in three days. The vessel had provisions of some kind on board, but everyone took a supply of oaten bread as well with them. The whole townland would be baking and hardening oaten bread for whoever was going away. They were baking for a fortnight beforehand. The bread would be hardened two or three times till you could walk on it. All the bread was packed in a small barrel that the coopers made for the purpose, and everyone going to America had his barrel. They used to get a *batáilte* [armful] of straw at Derry quay and a bag of biscuits for a shilling. That was how the O'Kanes made their money first, selling straw and biscuits at Derry quay, before they got into the whiskey trade. The straw was for sleeping on during the voyage.

Denis Harkin made a lot of money in Boston, but in 1857 he went to try his luck in California. At that time the journey had to be done by sea round South America. He had two companions with him by the name of Ward from the back country, and the three of them stayed at some hotel in California. One night Denis was attacked in bed and his throat cut, but he held the men and raised the alarm. When help came, who was it but the two Wards. There was a third man but he escaped out a window. Denis lived for four days and wrote a letter home, sitting up in his bed. The Wards were arrested, and the sheriff of the place said he would give Denis the privilege of inflicting whatever punishment he wished on the two of them. Denis said he was going where he'd be looking for forgiveness himself and to let them go.

All during my time people kept going to America and there's not a family in the parish but has somebody belonging to them in the States. There was always a big night for anybody going away. Neily McColgan, the blind fiddler, would be sent for, and they would dance till day-clearing. Then, too, for anyone coming home there was always a bottle-drink; but these led to so much drinking that Fr Fox put down the bottle-drinks entirely.

Most of them all got on well in the States. A relation of my mother's, the name of Diver, from Urris, went out before my time, and sure a grandson of his was made Governor of the State of Massachusetts in 1948.

Times at home were bad, and they left home with nothing but the clothes on their backs. The old people always said that good health and the grace of God were fortune enough for any young man or woman.

Chapter Seven

The Fair at Pollan

LONG AGO THERE WAS A GREAT FAIR held on Pollan
Green twice a year, the twenty-ninth of June and the tenth of
October. The last fair was held there on St Peter and Paul's Day in
the year of 1812. Before that it had been going on for hundreds of
years maybe. It was going strong in the time of the Bráthair na
Dumhcha [a famous local friar] and he died in 1784; and I heard
accounts of Colonel McNeill attending the fair of Pollan and he died
in 1709. From all accounts it must have been the greatest fair, maybe,
in the whole north of Ireland. The people gathered from all airts and
parts, and the green was black with people and standings and play-
actors of all kinds. It was a cattle, horse and sheep fair, but there was
great drinking and dancing and singing carried on, too. All the
mentioned girls of the three parishes were there, and many a match
and wedding was settled at the same fair of Pollan.

The cow-park was down at a place still called Garraí an Chladaigh,
and the sheep were kept in a field behind that called Áit an Aonaigh.
I often heard of a man who used to come with a horse and cart with
sweets and things, and on his way he kept shouting and singing: '*Tá
mé ag teacht, tá mé ag teacht go h-Aonach na bPollan* [I'm coming, I'm
coming to the fair of Pollan].'

All the old people had a song, too, about a boy who promised his
mother he'd do all the turns about the house, if she'd let him go to the
fair of Pollan:

Bhéarfaidh mé cnuasach chugat ón trá,
Crúbáin, creanach, duileasc breá;

Sníftdh mé iarna achan lá,
Ó a mhamaí lig mé chun aonaigh.
Cuirfidh mé an t-iarna ar an chrois,
Bogfaidh mé an cliabhán le mo chois,
Dheanfaidh mé garaíocht fríd an tí.
O a mhámaí lig me chun aonaigh.

[*I will bring you a hoard of food from the strand*
Crabs, shell dulse, sweet dulse;
I will spin a hank of yarn every day,
O, mammy, let me go to the fair.
I'll put the hank on the cross,
I'll rock the cradle with my foot,
I'll do all the wee jobs about the house.
O, mammy, let me go to the fair.]

Colonel McNeill was a bad man who lived at Binnion. He was a
Scotsman. He died in 1709. He likely got Binnion after the Reformation or after the Battle of the Boyne. I heard my father saying it was
people by the name of Toland who were driven out of Binnion when
it was taken over by McNeill. My father was at Carn fair one cold day
in winter, and there was an old Malin fisherman taking shelter from a
shower beside him. So my father remarked to him that this was a day
for a topcoat. The old man said if his people had their rights, it wasn't
one but two or three topcoats he could have, for it was his people who
owned Binnion in the old days. He was the name of Toland from
Ardmalin.

This Colonel McNeill had a very bad name and always kept a band
of henchmen or yeomen about him, who helped him to evict tenants
and seize girls and persecute the people. Some of them were from
Crossconnell, and some from Binnion.

There was an old woman called Máiread Dhubh who lived in a sod
house in Bunacrick moss with her four children. She caught salmon

during the summer-time to make a living and always went into the river and caught them with her hands. One day she was in the river down at Clochwan when McNeill and his men came on her, and with their swords and bayonets they kept her in the water till she was drowned. A Tanderagee man was going home from the Keelogs mill with a load of meal, and Máiread Dhubh called on him to save her but he drove on, and they say that Máiread cursed him and said the day would come when there wouldn't be one of his name in Tanderagee.

I heard that story told another way, where a man called Dochartach Mór na dTulcha was said to have killed Máiread Dhubh and that it wasn't McNeill at all.

Another time there was a funeral of some young woman who hadn't pleased Colonel McNeill. When they were carrying the coffin round Teampall Deas, McNeill and his men held up the funeral and took the lid off the coffin and put their swords through her. There was a girl about Crossconnell, too, and one night McNeill's men came to seize her, but she got out of bed and made up the side of Rachtan and got away on them.

Some of the women who had children to him got a rood of ground for their support. There was one of these roods in Gortnahinson, and some about Ballyliffin and different parts of the parish. The Ballyliffin Hotel is built on one of McNeill's roods. Some of his descendants were known in my young days, but I think they are all died out by now.

It was a common thing for women from the lower side of the parish to gather on the Binnion and Annagh hills and curse McNeill.

McNeill used to attend the fair of Pollan with his henchmen and pick out the best looking girl at the fair and carry her off to Binnion. One June fair they were taking a girl over the hill to Binnion, and when they were crossing behind Ardagh, Séimí Airis McCole heard her screaming and calling for help. Séimí was a mentioned man with the stick. He was hanging on a pot of potatoes at the time, so he called: '*Cá bhfuil mo bhataigín* [Where is my baton]?' and grabbed his stick and made out and jumped hedges and ditches till he overtook them about Mullach and fell to them with the stick till the girl got away.

Another fair of Pollan, a fine looking girl from Urris came in with her three brothers over through Annagh. When McNeill and his men went to seize the girl, she blew a birler, a kind of a whistle she carried, and it was heard all over the green. The brothers knew their sister's whistle and came to the rescue in time to save her. I heard, too, of a girl from Meentiagh Glen who went there for the first time. McNeill got his eye on her and arranged with her to meet him at six o'clock and that he'd leave her home on horseback. Some friends of hers warned her about the sort of a man he was and advised her to leave the fair at once and get home as hard as she could. She cut up through Tornabratly and over the side of Crockaughrim and got away home that way.

Things got so bad at the finish-up that some of the Ardagh men attacked McNeill one night at a place called Gallach in Annagh Hill, and felled him with a stone on the head, and Eoin Airis McCole castrated him with an old hook. His henchmen carried him home, and he lay for days before he died. The doctor maintained he would have recovered only for the blow on the head. I heard that the night he died he tore the side wall out of the house when the devil took him. The old people always said he was buried in the house at Binnion standing up, and that the corner where he is buried is built up. But there is a tombstone in the old churchyard at the corner facing Binnion with his name on it.

All the old people round this parish had a song about Pollan fair called 'Pléaráca na bPollan [Pollan Revels]'. Many a time I heard it sung. It was made by a brother of Dean O Donnell. He was Denis O Donnell and died in 1778. Dean O Donnell was parish priest here about two hundred years ago, before the Bráthair na Dumhcha. This is the song as far as I remember:

Éireoidh mé ar maidin is rachaidh mé chun aonaigh,
Tá mé 'mo chodladh is ná dúisítear mé.
Ligfidh mé le bradóg go bhfuil mé ar na daoraidh,
Tá mé 'mo chodladh is ná dúisítear mé.
Níl seascan bog baite nó áit a bhfuil pollóg ann,
Aniar ó Bhéal Trá go h-Árd na Cuileann Trá,
Nach mbímse seal sínte ar maos is mé ag ionfairt ann,
Tá mé 'mo chodladh is ná dúisítear mé.

Ag pilleadh aníos as Aonach na bPollan dom
Tá mé 'mo chodladh is ná dúisítear mé.
Le héirí na gealaí is le glaise na maidne,
Tá mé 'mo chodladh is ná dúisítear mé.
Cluinfear mo cheol mo ghlór is mo challán ann,
Carna mionna mór ar nós mar bhéadh dragan ann,
Chá dtéann tost ar mo scóig, ach ag ól, go rabh maidin ann,
Tá mé 'mo chodladh is ná dúisítear mé.

Ag dul thar an droichead ar dhéire mo phóiteacht,
Tá mé 'mo chodladh is ná dúisítear mé.
Fágfar céad crapán i mullach mo mhullaigh,
Tá mé 'mo chodladh is ná dúisítear mé.
Béidh mo hata's mo chóta síos liom 'na luideoga,
Mo charbhat is mo léine as a chéile 'na ribíní,
Is gur duibhe ná'n súiche mo ghuailne le greadóga
Tá mé 'mo chodladh is ná dúisítear mé.

Ag teacht bealach an tobair dom le stiúcadh mo scóige,
Tá mé 'mo chodladh is ná dúisítear mé.
Dheánfaidh mé scíste i dtí Shéamuis Uí Dhochartaigh,
Tá mé 'mo chodladh is ná dúisítear mé.
Chan fhágfaidh mé aon deor i soitheach a dearn cupaire,
Ó thoigh Bhillí Bháin go teach Éamoinn Chonnachtaigh,

Caithfidh mé an oíche le hÉamonn i gClocharna.
Tá mé 'mo chodladh is ná dúisítear mé.

[*I'll rise in the morning and go to the fair,*
I'm asleep and don't waken me.
I'll pretend to the girl that I'm in a mad fit,
I'm asleep and don't waken me.
There's not a marsh or a swamp or a bog-hole,
Across from Beltra to the height of Cullentree,
That I won't be steeped in and footering in,
I'm asleep and don't waken me.

On returning up from the fair of Pollan,
I'm asleep and don't waken me.
With the rise of the moon and the breaking of dawn,
I'm asleep and don't waken me.
My singing and shouting and noise will be heard there,
Heaps of big curses as if 'twas a dragon,
My throat will not silence, except while drinking, till the morning,
I'm asleep and don't waken me.

Going over the bridge at the end of my spree,
I'm asleep and don't waken me.
There will be hundreds of lumps on the top of my head,
I'm asleep and don't waken me.
My hat and my coat will be around me in tatters,
My scarf and my shirt will be sundered in ribbons
And my shoulders black as soot with batterings and blows,
I'm asleep and don't waken me.

Coming over past the well, and my throat parching,
I'm alseep and don't waken me.
I will rest a while with Séamus O Doherty,

I'm asleep and don't waken me.
I won't leave a drop in any vessel ever a cooper made,
From Billy Ban's house to the tent of Éamonn the Connachtman,
Then I'll spend the night with Éamonn in Clogherna,
I'm alseep and don't waken me.]

Chapter Eight

Poets, Publicans and Pilgrimages

DENIS O DONNELL, THE POET, DIED in 1778 and was buried in the old graveyard in Straid. The tombstone is there yet. There was a descendant of his, Hudy Aodh Rua, who was a very educated man. He could read your hand and could tell from the air what kind of a season was coming. He got his knowledge from books he had. He had books in Irish and in English and some book called *Aristotle*.

There was a young fellow one time who was going to get married and had the day fixed and all. So he went to Hudy to get his hand read. When Hudy finished without any mention of the wedding, the fellow told him that he'd have to stop his nonsense, for that he was going to get married on such a day. Hudy looked at his hand again and told him the marriage thread was not in his hand. On the day he was to be married the young fellow was buried.

One warm day in June crowds of people were in the moss cutting turf. Hudy told all hands to leave and make for home at once or the floods would take them before they got home. Nobody listened to him, but late in the afternoon the rain started and they were nearly swept out of the moss.

Most of the old books were lost, and many of them were burned during outbreaks of fever for fear of spreading the disease. One of these old books of Hudy's is still in Hugh O Donnell's in Rooskey. It deals with the sun, moon and stars, but is written in difficult Irish and is very hard to make out.

Many of the old people were good at forecasting the weather or noticing a change coming. I wasn't a bad hand at it myself. I would notice signs like the cobwebs on the whins, or a blue blaze in the embers, or the way the smoke goes up from the chimney, or the noise of the water in the brook. After a dry spell, when the brook sounds noisy, the old people would say that the river was laughing for rain.

I heard accounts of a man called Seán Mac an Meirge who lived about Malin and the Isle of Doagh two or three hundred years ago. His real name was Doherty, and there was a time when he owned several quarterlands in Malin and the Isle of Doagh. He lived at Keenagh in Malin. He had two sons. One of them was a major in King James's army, and fought with James at the Boyne. One of the daughters had a bit of land about Malin. One time she was in Derry and a packman offered her £50 for her share, but she wouldn't take it. Then he offered her a silk dress along with the £50 and they closed the bargain at that. He was a packman who went round peddling linen yarn and silk and things like that. When he got the place in Malin, he opened a shebeen. Seán Mac an Meirge was his best customer for he was fond of the drink. Instead of paying for the drink, Seán ran up bills, and the packman kept a tally. There was a river between Seán's house and the shebeen, and the packman always carried him across on his back. One day when Seán signed to be carried over, he paid no heed to him. Seán called across: "Why aren't you coming to carry me over?' The packman called back to him: 'You have no more land left to drink; it's all mine now.'

Seán Mac an Meirge was some relation of the Bráthair na Dumh-cha. Seán was a sort of poet, too, but went to the bad with drink. The old people had a song of his but I remember only a bit of it:

Dúirt Colmcille gur go h-Ifrinn go bráth nach dtéadh an fial,
Lucht na h-ircise go milleann siad a bpáirt le Dia.
Gur mhór an tubaiste do dhuine ar bith a dearn ariamh é
Oiread cruinniú a dhéanamh is choinneodh as Parrthas é.

Nuair a gheobhas mise bás, gheobhaidh mé ciste beag den bhord.
Chá ngeobhann muintir an tsaibhrís mórán mór den tseort.

[*Colmcille said that the generous-hearted man would never go to Hell,*
But that misers cut themselves off from God.
He said that it is a great misfortune for a person
To gather a hoard of wealth that would keep him out of Paradise.
When I die I will get a small wooden coffin.
Wealthy people won't get much more.]

There was another song of his that he made when he was an old
man and had fallen into poverty and want. I heard it sung many a
time:

Is mé an creatúir tinn tolglach ar an mhullach ansiud thall,
Níl duine le m'fhiafraí anois go luath nó go mall.
Dá mbéadh spré caoraigh, ba is capaill agamsa le roinn
Bhéadh go leor ansin a deirfeadh: 'Muise, a Sheáin, tá tú tinn.'

Ach go mbreachtar mo mhalaidhe is go liathar mo cheann
Comh geal leis an eala ar an chnoc is ar linn,
Go dtéidh mo bhean sa talamh is indiaidh í féin a clann,
Béidh mo dhúil 'sna cannaí is go síorraí ins an dram.

[*I'm a sickly poor creature living on the height over there,*
Without anyone to ask about me early or late.
If I had a stock of sheep, cattle, and horses to share out
There would be many to say to me 'Indeed, Seán, you're sick.'

But till my brows and hair turn white
Like the swan on hill or pond,
Till my wife goes to her grave and after her her family,
I will always love the spirits and forever the dram.]

I think it would be a descendant of these Dohertys of Keenagh who was a great harp player, the best in Ireland. One Christmas market he was going to the fair of Carn, but his stepmother, who could *spey* [foresee] and read the planets, advised him not to go for there was blood over his head. When he insisted on going, she killed a rooster and sprinkled the blood over him. On his way into the town, a row got up between a crowd of Catholics and a crowd of Protestants, so Doherty joined in, too, and stabbed an Orangeman, so he had to clear out of the country and was never seen back again.

Down at Pollan strand in the old days there was a public house and it's likely poteen would be plentiful. The wallsteads of the public house are there yet. A woman named Síle an Chladaigh used to run it, and she got married to a man called Charles McNulty who came from Kilmacrennan direction. It seems Síle was gong to America and fell in with McNulty about Derry while they were waiting for a boat to sail. He was for America, too. Anyhow, they struck up and got married and never went any further. They came back and the two of them ran the public house in Pollan. He was a shoemaker to trade and was called Brógaí [Shoes] for a nickname. They made a right living between the public house and the shoemaking. He used to keep a donkey for taking down the barrels of whiskey and beer from the road at Ballyliffin. He was very strict about the public house. He had the name of putting water in the whiskey and used to say to his customers: 'Don't be afraid to drink your fill; there is nothing in it but the blessed water from the *turas* [pilgrimage].'

People played tricks on Brógaí. One night three Rashenny fellows came in with a rabbit skin to sell. They got half-a-pint for the skin. The light was bad, so the second fellow lifted the skin when Brógaí's back was turned and sold it to him again for another half-pint. The third fellow did the same.

The McNultys had one daughter, Síle, and she married Billy Hegarty of Ardagh. Billy had a brother, Fr Charles Hegarty, who was educated in Paris, but took a very short life with him and died when he was twenty-nine. He was the first to be buried in the present grave-yard in 1820.

Ballyliffin was a growing place at that time, and the Ballyliffin people wanted the fair changed up there from Pollan Green. When the Pollan fair day of the tenth of October 1812 came round, a crowd of Ballyliffin men gathered at Tochar to turn everybody up from going over the green and head them for Ballyliffin. Brógaí went over to clear the road to Pollan, and a fight soon started. They were too many for Brógaí, and they gave him such abuse that he had to be carried home on a door. He took to his bed and died shortly after. They fought with sticks, and Brógaí maintained that if he had one man to stand behind him he would have cleared the road. Years after it used to be a password with the John Wright's Men [faction fighters], 'Who killed Brógaí?'

The fair was held in Ballyliffin after that and the cow-park was up where the station-house is now. The fair of Ballyliffin was held on the same dates as the old fair of Pollan. The tenth of October fair was a great one entirely. The young people would rise out from all parts, and in my father's time it was the greatest fair from Derry down. Drink was for next to nothing, and they were fighting and sledging and felling one another. Men carried short sticks up the sleeves of their coats till the row would start. Sometimes the women would hold the men's coats, and they used to shout to their men: *'Tabhair dó é* [Give it to him]!'

Public houses from the Cross to Carn or Buncrana could put up a signboard and get a licence for the day. Nearly every house in Bally-liffin was a public house for that day. And with the price of drink a man could get drunk on three half-pence, I always heard. The story was often told of two Tullagh men who went to the holiday fair of Carn with sixpence each. They came back at night-fall, roaring drunk, and had lots of money home with them.

That time whiskey was a penny a glass. After the Crimea War it went up to a shilling for the half-pint. For a while everybody stopped drinking with whiskey at that price, but they were as bad as ever again in no time.

In later years the police opened a barracks at Ballyliffin for the fair days. It was in the house where McLaughlin's shop is now. In times ago there was a lot of party trouble and many a man got a beating at the fair of Ballyliffin that he didn't get over. The people would have daylight with them coming home in the morning.

I was at the fair at Ballyliffin myself and saw cattle at it. But it was dying out at that time and stopped altogether when the fair was changed to the Cross.

Ballyliffin must have been a place in times ago. Down at the strand there is a *turas* that all the old people used to make on the first Monday of August. My father and mother made it often and I made it myself a time or two. There are five beds of stones and you go round the first bed seven times and say an Our Father and seven Hail Marys. Under the waterfall is a holy well called Tobar Muiris, or some people called it Tobar Mac Muiris. After going round the beds you went to the shore and dipped your hand into the first three waves and threw the water over your shoulder in the name of the Father and of the Son and of the Holy Ghost and made a cross on your forehead with the water. Going round the beds you always started at your right-hand side and went round that way.

Round the face of Binnion Hill there's a cave, and nobody knows how far in its goes. Long ago a piper went in there to find out where it led to or what was in it. He arranged with his friends that he would keep playing and they could listen above the ground and find out the direction the cave went. They traced him with the playing of the pipes till he was over under lower Annagh. The tune he was playing was:

Béidh na cailíní óga ina seanmhná
Sul a bhfille mé, sul a bhfille mé.

Béidh na huain óga ina seanchaoraigh,
Nuair a thiocfas mise arais.

[*The young girls will be old women*
Before I return, before I return.
The young lambs will be old sheep
Before I come back again.]

They lost track of the piper after that and he never came back. The cave is called Poll an Phíobaire [The Piper's Cave] since that time.

On that side of Binnion Hill is Beann an Eibhir [Granite Cliff] and beside it is a spot called Copanna Chonnla [Connla's Cups]. They say there was a giant in the olden times by the name of Connla, and that he has crocks of gold buried there that were never discovered and that was how it got its name. But they say there's gold hidden at the Turas rocks, too, and a crock of gold buried under the Carthach stone in Clogherna.

Chapter Nine

The Parish

THIS PARISH TOOK ITS NAME FROM a small three-cornered piece of ground out beside the old church in Straid. That was likely the place where the old monastery was built long ago. It must have dated from the time of St Colmcille for there is a rock in the old graveyard with the track of his two knees in it. I often heard of people being cured by rubbing the water in those two holes on whatever part was sore, in the name of the Father and of the Son and of the Holy Ghost.

Near that piece of ground there is a height called Drom na Scolb, and the old people said that was the place the monks used to dry the briars when they would be thatching the monastery. It was a thatched roof was on it. The monastery well was in one of the tree corners, the one next to the church wall. There is not a trace of the monastery left now, although at one time three-hundred-and-fifty monks lived there.

The family of the Muirgheasans must have had something to do with the monastery, for there is a height in their farm called Teampall Deas, and at funerals the corpse was carried round that height three times, before it was taken to the old graveyard. My grandfather was taken round the height when he died in 1840, and lots of others since then, till people stopped burying there.

The monastery must have been destroyed between 1600 and 1700 for there was a minister here with a Protestant church about 1700. The present church, now in ruins, was built in 1801 by masons named Thomas. The first minister I heard of was Donal McLoughlin who died in 1711. He had a brother, Peadar, who was parish priest here at the same time. The old people had a lot of stories about these two brothers.

They were from Gleneely and were going abroad for their education when their ship was wrecked. They were rescued by a Protestant gentleman they fell in with who offered to educate them if they turned. Donal agreed and later became the Protestant rector of Clonmany and built Dresden. Peadar refused and continued to the continent where he was ordained and became parish priest of Clonmany. He lived somewhere about Crossconnell.

Their old mother came out to see them one time and to try and get Donal to come back to his faith. But he only mocked her. He was holding a service in the church at Straid when she put her head in the door. As soon as he saw her he went down the floor to meet her. She made out the door again, and he called after her: '*A mháthair, rith, rith, no béirfidh an diabhal ort* [Mother, run, run, or the devil will catch you]!'

Early in the penal times, shortly after 1700, there was a Fr McColgen who served this parish and the most of Inishowen. He was on his banishment, and one time he called at a certain house for something to eat. It was run by Protestants, but the servant girl was a Catholic. She wanted to give the priest a hint to clear out and wait for nothing. So as she was roasting a herring she tried to warn him of the danger he was in, by saying: '*Cuimhnigh ar an scadán, nar gabhadh ariamh le baoite* [Remember the herring that was never caught with bait].' He didn't take her up, so after a minute or two she got a chance and whispered: '*Ma's maith leat bhéith buan cáith uait agus teich* [If you want to remain alive, throw all from you and flee].' He made off without waiting for anything to eat, and before the herring was roasted on the other side, the place was surrounded by yeomen. It was at some seaside place this happened, for the yeomen put stones through the bottom of all the boats for fear he'd get away that way. Only for the girl Fr McColgan would have been captured.

At this time, of course, there was no chapel or place to say Mass in, except at the Mass rocks about the hills. There are Mass rocks in every part of this parish. There's Leac na hAltóra, Garrdha an tSagairt, the Altar Rock, Leac an Aifrinn and as many more. The priests had no settled way on them till about 1780 or so, till Fr Corr came here in 1784. Before that time wandering friars went about and said Mass here and there about the hills. The people would get word beforehand where to go. I heard that a Fr Maginn used to say Mass at the Altar Rock above in Butler's Glen. He came from Donagh on horseback. He would be an uncle or granduncle of Dr Maginn, afterwards parish priest of Buncrana and later bishop of Derry.

It was before 1784 that the friars went about. They were a droll lot of men, and I heard old rhymes about them arguing and bantering and joking with the people. One old rhyme I heard mentioned two of them by name, Friar McLaughlin and Friar McEgan. This is it:

Arsa'n Bráthair 'Ac Lachlainn ar a dhul thart dó:
'Téigí chun Aifrinn amárch.'
Arsa'n Bráthair 'Ac Aodhagain lena chuid gaoithe:
'Bíodh mhúr m-iarna snáith libh.'
'Chan fhánn tú aon iarna uaimsa i mbliana,
Chan fhánn tú aon iarna amháin uaim.
Deamhan an iarna a ghéibh tú i mbliana,
Is mór an cíos na bráithre.
Chá dtéimsa chun Aifrinn go cionn bliana
Ach rachaidh mé chun an teampaill,
An áit a gcluinfidh mé na bréaga.'
Arsa'n Bráthair leis ansin:
'Coinnigh do iarna a Mhanuis!'

[*Said Friar McLaughlin on his rounds,*
'Everybody for Mass tomorrow.'
Said Friar McEgan in his breezy way,

'And bring along your hanks of yarn.'
Manus replied:
'You'll get no hank from me this year,
Not a single one.
The friars have us taxed too heavily
I'll go to no Mass for a year
But I will go to the church
Where I'll hear all the lies!'
Then the Friar said,
'Keep your hank, Manus!']

Another time one of the friars called in some house over about Rashenny:

Arsa'n bráthair: 'Cá bhfuil do mháthair?'
'Chuaidh sí anonn go Rúscaí,
Ag rith, ag reath, ag iarraidh dath,
Le cuir ar stocaí domh-sa.'
'Bhí rith ina tóin, an chailleach bheag chróin,
Na nar fhan sa bhaile ag a túirne.
Tá níos mó luaithe buí fá dtaobh den tí,
Ná a chuirfeadh dath ar ghúna.'

[*Said the friar: 'Where's your mother?'*
'She went over to Rooskey,
Running and rushing,
To look for dye for my stockings.'
'She was always a runner, the yellow hag.
Can't she stay at home at her spinning wheel?
There's more ashes about this house
Than would dye a whole dress.']

The best known of all the friars was the Bráthair na Dumhcha. He was also called the Bráthair Dubh, the Black Friar, and lived about

Carraig a' Brachaí and the Isle of Doagh. He was the parish priest before Fr Corr, and died in 1784.

The owner of Carraig a' Brachaí years ago was Donnchadh Mór an Chaisleáin, the late Patrick Quigley's grandfather. The Bráthair na Dumhcha was an uncle to this Donnchadh Mór O Dochartaigh. It appears that three brothers of them were friars. One of them was martyred in the Diamond of Derry, another was professor in the Irish college in Louvain, and the third was the Bráthair na Dumhcha, the Bráthair Dubh O Dochartaigh, who belonged to the Dominican order.

All the old people had a song about the Bráthair na Dumhcha that he composed himself, and it used to be sung at big nights and weddings and bottle-drinks all over the parish. There's nobody living now has the song but myself. This is it:

Baile'n Mhullaigh os cionn Arda, is aoibhinn áluinn bárr na mbeann.
Tífea Iorrus uait is Malainn, Cnoc na Dála is iomaí am.
I gCreig a' Bhainne, Lag, is Craonach, Glac na Bradach, sin is Drung,
Lag a' Churraigh, Coill, is Clara, is thiar in Eanach a d'ól mé dram.

'Sa Carraig a'Bhrachaí bhí mé céad uair, insna méilte seala ag ól,
Ag an Chaisleán b'fhada luigh mé ann, is ar Oileán Glas Éidigh ba bhinn
*   mo ghlór.*
Bhí mé ag iascaireact ar Tráigh Bréige is in Rath Síonnaigh a ghabhainn
*   ceol.*
Shnámh mé an Fhairrge go dtí an Bréidin is shíl na céadtaí nach rabh mé
*   beo.*

Bhí mé ar meisce i gCnoc na Gaoithe agus 'mo shuidhe aréir go mall.
As sin thuas go Gleann na Mínteach annsin orm féin a rinneadh an
*   fheall.*
Bhí cúpla buidéal de'n spiorad-sa uaim, bhí siad líonta annsin,

Ach dubhairt fear acu a bhí ró chríonna an rabh an phighinn os cionn mo gheall.

Le h-éirighe gealaighe bhí mé in ordú is gan aon fheoirling agam le díol.
Fuair mé mo chasóg is mo chlóca na luighe síos stroctha ag mo thaobh.
Leán mé cailín a ghoid mo bhróga uaim ach d'imthigh sí romham sa bhogach bhuidhe.
D'éirigh an baile, lean an tóir mé, is sheol mé romham mar bád na gaoithe.

Cuaidh mé go Rúscaí ionnsair Gráinne, chá dtabharfadh sí carta ar mo scór.
Chá raibh agam ach sean-wig is hata gránna, d'fhág mé ar lár iad is bhuail mé an bórd.
Dúirt sí liom a dhul chun siúl, is níor chuir sí áird ar mo ghlór.
Ach d'ól mé buidéal ar an Sráid, tuilleadh is mo sháith ar an Mhachaire Mhór.

D'fhoghlaim mé Laidin is Gréigís, i bhfad anois is mé ag dul annon.
Ba dheas mo charbhat is siúd mo léine ag toigh Sheárlais in Árd a' Chrainn.
Bhí mé iln Arda 'mach ag imirt cárdaí, d'ól mé sláinte Eoghain Uí Neill,
Ar mo theacht anuas ar an Mhachaire Árd, bhí mé lá na rásaí le Máire Bhaird.

I mBaile Challain as sin go h Eachraim, ba mhian liom ag déanaumh poit,
In Inis Eoghain gan stad nó scíste i bhfad san oíche is mé ag déanamnh ceoil.
Bailte beaga is bailte móra, san chuid is mo acú ó Dhoire anuas,
Ach Ceathrú Trasna is íoctar Fanaid, sin dhá áit nach rabh mé ariamh.

The words of the song are hard to make out in places, but it goes someway like this:

In the town of Mullach above Ardagh, it is pleasant on top of the bens.
You can see Urris and Malin and Crucknadala many a time.
In Creigaweny, Lagg and Creenagh, Glacknabrada from there to Drung,
Lagahurry, Coill and Clara, and over in Annagh I drank a drop.

In Carrickabraghy I was a hundred times and through the sandbanks
*   drinking,*
Down at the Castles I often lay, and out on Glashedy Island my voice was
*   sweet.*
I was often fishing on Trabreigy and in Rashenny I often sang.
I swam the sea of the Breidin and hundreds thought that I was drowned.

I was drunk in Crucknagee and was up late last night.
Then I went up to the Glen of Meentiagh and it was there I was treated
*   foul.*
I wanted a couple of bottles of spirits, they were filled there on the spot,
But the man of the house who was over-wise asked had I the money
*   fornenst my shout.*

When the moon got up I was in order but hadn't a farthing on me to pay,
Then I found my coat and my cloak lying torn at my side.
I followed a girl who stole my shoes from me but she made off across the
*   bog.*
Then the town rose out and the chase came after me, but I sailed on ahead
*   like a boat before the wind.*

I went to Rooskey, over to Grainne's but she would not give me a quart on
*   credit.*
I had nothing but an old wig and a battered hat, so I threw them down
*   and rapped the table again.*
But she paid no heed to me and told me to be off.
However I got a bottle out in Straid and then my fill and more up in
*   Magheramore.*

*I learned Latin and Greek many years ago now, for I'm getting on in
years.*
I had fine clothes at that time in Charley's house in Ardacrann.
*I was in Ardagh playing cards, and drank a health to Owen O Neill,
And coming down through Maghera Ard I spent the day of the races with
Mary Ward.*

*In Ballyhallion and up at Aughrim, I always liked to go on a spree,
Through Inishowen without stop or stay, far into the night and I singing
my fill.*
*Small towns and big towns, in most of them all from Derry down,
Except Carrowtrasna and the bottom of Fanad—two places I was
never in.*

When Fr Corr came here as parish priest in the year 1784, the
persecutions must have been past, for at that time Mass was said for
the whole parish at a place above Andy Porters called the Scallan.
Near it is a height called Ard na hEaglaise—the Chapel Height. The
corner stones of the Scallan are there yet. It was a kind of a shelter, for
I always heard there was a big sheet of cloth put up on whatever side
the wind was coming from, to give shelter to the altar. People came to
the Scallan from all ends of the parish, and all the men took their
*camán*s [hurley sticks], and when Mass was over someone threw out
the *cnag* [ball] and one side of the parish played the other, the Isle of
Doagh side against the Urris side. Each side tried to take the *cnag*
home, and they played through fields and everything, and the side
that took home the *cnag* had the game won. There was no prize or
anything. *Camán* was the whole game before this. It was the common
game till about forty or fifty years ago.

When Fr Shiels came here from Cloncha in 1794, after Fr Corr
died, he set about building the present chapel. Lots of people wanted
the chapel built at the Scallan in Gaddyduff but Fr Shiels picked the
place where the chapel stands now. The old people always called the

priests Sagart Corr and Sagart Síadhail, Priest Corr and Priest Shiels. The chapel was built in 1795 and enlarged in 1829. With the extensions and building, the chapel was badly in debt in Fr O Donnell's time. The collection at the chapel gate wasn't amounting to much, so Fr O Donnell put a levy of a guinea on every house in the parish, and the whole debt was cleared in a fortnight.

When the bishop came to bless the bell, there was such a crowd that half of them couldn't get into the chapel, so the bishop put them all out to the yard, and spoke to them through the window. He said the bell would be heard seven miles away, and when the devil heard it, he would fly. The bell was rung on the ninth of April 1845, and that was the first Catholic bell to be heard in this parish from the time of the Reformation. But with all kinds of people ringing it, the bell got cracked and a new bell was got in 1870. It wasn't rung during frost for fear of cracking it. Phil Bhriney and Donal Fad hoisted the bell up to the tower. Fr McCullagh promised them that the bell would be rung free for them at their own funerals.

In 1829 Fr Shiels died, and he was succeeded by Fr O Donnell, the Waterloo priest, who was parish priest here till 1856. Then came Fr John Doherty, but he took a short life, and died two years later. Fr John McLaughlin of Tornabratly was parish priest then from 1858 to 1873. He was succeeded by Fr William Doherty who lived till 1900, and then Fr Maguire became parish priest. Fr Maguire spent his whole life in this parish, coming here as curate in 1878 after his ordination in Rome, and remaining here till he died parish priest in 1933.

I do not remember so much about the curates of the parish. Fr Corr, who succeeded the Bráthair na Dumhcha in 1784, had no curate at all. Some of the wandering friars may have helped him now and again. In Fr Corr's time the ghost of Archie Rua had everyone about the parish frightened. He was seen driving two black horses up the Pinch road at night. That was the main road to Derry in times gone by. One night Fr Corr was coming from a sick call, and Archie appeared and galloped home with him till they reached Fr Corr's door. At that time Fr Corr lived with the Grants at Magheracarry in Annagh. He had the best black horse ever you saw on four feet, and when they reached home that night, the horse was as white as a swan in his own sweat. The Grants heard the galloping and guessed that Archie was afoot, so they closed the stable door. Only for that the horse would have rushed in and crushed the priest on the door-head.

Archie Rua was a tithe-proctor by the name of McLucas. One time he put a gallon keg of poteen to his head at the Keelogs mill and drank it till he burst himself. That was the way he died. His ghost was often seen after it, galloping about on horseback after night and hunting with dogs through the mills. The old people used to say that he tossed their footings of turf in the moss. He used to live at the Bridge House and drank the poteen because some girl turned him down. But the night he went home with the priest, Fr Corr handed him a pass, and that confined him to some one place, and he never bothered anybody after.

Fr Shiels took over Termain and built the big house that is there yet about the year 1820 or so. In order to make up the farm seven families had to be evicted. He helped at the evictions himself, too. I heard that he evicted one family after he had said Mass and before he took his breakfast; and he even carried out a cradle with an infant in it and left it on the street. The old people didn't want to talk about it. The place afterwards fell to a niece of his who married Owen Doherty, a son of Niall Seán's. Termain was a place that nobody ever thrived in. There was always a writ or a subpoena hanging over it.

Fr Shiels served the parish alone for seven years till Friar Higgins came and during all that time there wasn't one ever died without the priest. Fr Shiels was very great with a landlord who owned the Glen House and a lot of quarterlands in this parish and had thirty-two quarterlands in the county of Armagh. The old people called this man the Dalach Rua, so he must have been named O Donnell. They also spoke of him as Mac an tSagart Francach, for he was the son of a French priest who turned to be a Protestant. He used to come from Armagh on his holidays to the Glen House, and his daughter had a bathing-box down at the strand. Years later when a son of his inherited the estate, after the Dalach Rua died, the young fellow fell to drink and went to the bad completely. He ended up penniless and died in a sod house somewhere about Armagh. The old people always had a saying: 'The son's son suffers for the wrong done.' The Dalach Rua was a man had great power. They say he could take a man from the scaffold.

It was the Dalach Rua who offered Fr Shiels any part of his lands that he cared to pick to build a house on. Fr Shields selected a spot beyond the Glen House where a man called Seán Jack lived. One day he called and told Seán to drive his pigs out of there, that he wanted the place for a house. But Seán Jack followed him with a graip and hunted them. The next place he put his eye on was Termain.

At some period Fr Shiels had Termain House let to the soldiers at a rent of £8 a year.

A few years ago Rev. Dr Gallagher showed me a small Mass bell that was found in a tree in Termain. It was a brass bell with a staple on top of it for a handle. It likely belonged to Fr Shiels for he was the only priest who lived there. In his time the Protestant minister was the Rev. Chichester, and in his last illness Fr Shiels called to see him every day. He attended the funeral too, and when the coffin was passing him in the church door, Fr Shiels reached over and cut the sign of the cross on the side of the coffin. People said that Rev. Chichester died a Catholic. He died in 1815. The Chichesters left Dresden in 1826.

The first curate I heard of coming to Clonmany was a Fr Paul Bradley in the last years of Fr Shiels's time. He lived in a house in Tirberry. The house is still standing but it is used as a sheep *cró* [fold]. Billy Bán McCarron's mother was keeping house to Fr Shiels at the time Fr Bradley came, and on his first Sunday here I believe he preached a great sermon entirely. Everybody spoke about the good luck the parish had to get such a fine speaker. Fr Shiels passed the remark to Billy's mother that it was all the worse for them; that now when they knew the rules of religion, they would have to live up to them.

Fr Shiels would let nobody be buried in the new graveyard attached to the chapel until he would die himself. But it happened different to what Fr Shiels planned. Fr Hegarty of Ardagh died before him, and his was the first grave to be opened.

Round about that same time, Fr Porter of Ballintleve was curate in Malin. He was there the year of the Dear Summer in 1817, and times were so bad he had to come home for he couldn't get his support in Malin. My father said the Dear Summer was a worse famine in places then the Famine of 1847. In 1817 the potatoes failed and there was no Indian meal coming in at that time for relief. It wasn't allowed in till after the Free Trade Bill was passed during the Famine of '47. Fr Porter stayed at home all week and would leave Ballintleve on horseback and take a lunch of oaten bread with him on Sunday morning and say Mass in Malin and come home that night. Later on he became parish priest of Malin.

I heard the time he was there that he had an outfall with a woman in Malin about a cotter tenant that was in a cottage of his. She said she wouldn't be ruled by a priest. She was well off and had twenty-eight head of cattle, four working horses and £1,100 in the bank. Fr Porter said Charity was her name and that she'd be a charity herself before long, and that there would be briars growing on her headstone before seven years. Before that time was up, she went down in the world and the place was sold in Carn courthouse for £80 of debt. It went for £200. The man who bought the place didn't need the house and took the roof off it. When his men were cleaning out the place they came on a briar growing in the old fireplace with three green leaves on it.

The Waterloo priest, Fr O Donnell, came home from the wars the same time as my grandfather got out of the navy. He had two brothers priests but they were ordained and dead before he was ordained in 1818. The three brothers are buried in the one grave at Cock Hill.

The Waterloo priest was a fine upstanding man and a great horseman. He had a big chestnut horse home with him from the battle of Waterloo and he called him Paddy Whack. He lived at Crossconnell and later on at the Cross. One day one of the redcoats was passing and struck Fr O Donnell's dog with his whip. When the housekeeper gave off to him about it, the soldier said he'd do the same to the dog's master. When she told Fr O Donnell, he put on his uniform and jumped on Paddy Whack and overtook the redcoat at the Carry Hole near Buncrana and made him go down on his knees on the roadside and apologise.

There was a mark of a wound on the horse's hip and the story was that during the wars they ran short of food and cut a piece off the horse to eat.

Fr O Donnell spent a quarter in Lifford jail one time for not paying tithes. When he was released, the whole parish turned out to meet him out of face. It was the Glen House people who put him to jail. So he made a speech to the crowd out there and said the day would come when there would not be one of the Glen House breed in this parish.

Fr William O Donnell came here as curate after his ordination in 1841. He was from Glenmahee and was a nephew of the Waterloo priest. He wasn't the same O Donnells; a sister's son, I think. He had a brother a doctor and another brother, Dominic, who lived at Cock Hill. He spent his whole curacy in this parish, and left here in 1868 to become a parish priest. He lived in a house in Gortnahinson. The wallsteads are there yet. He worked the farm and had a working horse and kept a boy. All the priests before this had land and worked it. Fr O Donnell went in greatly for cattle and used to send cattle for grazing to Neall Dhiarmada in Effishmore during the summertime. It was this Fr O Donnell who attended my uncle Owen when he died in 1842. There was another Fr O Donnell here before that as a curate, for it was a curate of that name who baptised Phil Bhriney, and Phil got the pension the first day it came out in 1908, which would mean that he was born in 1838.

All the noted singers were in the choir that time. They had no harmonium and the music they had was fiddles and flutes. John McEleney of Ballinabo was master of the choir and would point out the notes with a pencil. Billy Andy Porter of Gaddyduff used to play the fiddle. Away back in Fr Shiels's time, about 1820 and before, it was all flutes they had. Séamus Aindrias McCool and his brother Charley played the flutes at that time. They were great singers, too. The Harkins of Clogherna had music in them. Music is a thing that follows tribes of people.

This parish always had a Protestant minister from the time of the Reformation up to 1873. The last was the Rev. Thompson who lived at Dunally, the Glebe House. The Rev. Chichester lived at Dresden and I heard of the Rev. Laing who lived in Bocharna and was choked by same fresh butter and oaten bread that went with his breath. The Rev. Dobbs was here between 1830 and 1840.

About the time I was born there was a man who lived in Meentiagh Lodge named Gibbs. He was married to one of the Harveys, the landlords, and he and Mrs Gibbs used to go round visiting people in the Glen and gave presents of tea to people they were great with. Gibbs was not a clergyman but he was always talking about points of religion and arguing to show that Catholics were idolators. He was very good if there was a sickness in a house and as good as a doctor for people that had the fever. People took the tea but that was as far as it went. The priests were against people taking presents from them.

Fr John Doherty of Ballyliffin was the first parish priest to set up in the present parochial house in the year 1856. The place belonged to Termain and the house at that time was an ordinary one-storey with kitchen and two rooms, slated with slates from McDaids' quarry on Ballintleve Hill. The same slates were on the scutch-mill and the meal-mill there. Fr Doherty took a short life: he died in 1858. The present house was built by Fr William Doherty in 1877 but there was a range of office houses there with thatched roofs in my own time.

Before Fr John Doherty's time the land with house and office houses was offered to a man for £17 but he didn't take it.

Chapter Ten

Cures and Spells

IN THE OLDEN TIMES THERE WERE FEW ailments in man or beast that the old people hadn't a cure for. They worked greatly with herbs and old Dr McEleney of Tullagh said there was a cure of some kind in every plant that grows if people only knew it. Some of the cures they went in for were only *pisreog* [superstitious] cures that did neither good nor harm. People only laugh at them now.

Very few people going now know how to make the cure for the 'rose' [erysipelas]. Ann Roddy was a good hand at it and so was Hudy Bán McEleney and lots more. Donal Roddy learned how to make it from Eoin O Kerrigan himself. Eoin said there were nine different kinds of the 'rose' and the poultice was made up of nine different things—the root of the stinking roger, a rose noble, the daisy plant roots and leaves, fern leaves, docken leaves, primrose leaves and woodbine leaves, and pennywort leaves. These were all grounded together and heated in a pot and then the poultice was ready. Dr Thompson, nephew of Rev. Thompson, had great belief in the cure and had all the herbs growing in his garden.

There's a small bush called the *gibire gearr* [probably a type of juniper] that grows in dry hilly places. It burns like fir in the fire when it's withered. The she-kind has green berries all over it but the he-kind has no berries at all. They say if the berries and leaves are boiled the water is good for people that are run down or have bad blood. They mend well after it. There is great virtue in the broom, too. If the tops of the branches are boiled they are a great cure for dropsy or swelling that would come from the kidneys. There is a he-kind and a she-kind of broom, too. Another great cure for kidney trouble was *ruid-eagach* [bog-myrtle] and it was used like the broom. *Grúnlas* [groundsel] heated over the fire and applied like a poultice gave great ease in cases of gravel. *Crann cuinse* [quince] was good for healing the inside. *Fanann*, or coltsfoot, was good for a cough, and I heard of *fearaban*, or crowfoot, being used as a poultice but I forget what it was for.

People before this used to smoke mugweed leaves and as far as I remember it was for people that lost the appetite. They smoked it in a pipe like tobacco.

For cuts and sores I often used St Patrick's leaf or, as some people call it, the healing leaf. You just chewed it up and put it on the cut. A cobweb on a bleeding cut helped the blood to freeze and stopped the bleeding.

If there was a bealing or a stony bruise that needed drawing, the leaf of the foxglove warmed over a coal drew out whatever poison was in it. The *boglas* leaf [ox-tongue herb] was used in the same way. The lick of a dog's tongue was good for a cut or a sore that wasn't healing up right. There's a cure on the dog's tongue. The fox's tongue was supposed to have great drawing powers. When a fox was caught, somebody always wanted the tongue. At a time when pigs or cattle were killed, the bladder was blown up and dried, and there's nothing better for a cut heel or toe than a piece of the pig's bladder. Oak bark was a great cure for sore feet. The bark was steeped in water for a day or two and the water was good for hardening the skin of the feet in the summer-time.

In my young days every house pulled bogbine in the spring-time. It was for the bogbine roots, and they were boiled and mixed with treacle and sulphur. This was a well-tried remedy for purifying the blood. The blood gets out of order in the spring-time. Bogbine is used till the present day.

I heard of women stewing the tea-plant the same way as you'd make tea. It grows on the roadside with a puce flower. It was used for growing girls that weren't too strong and that might take the decline [tuberculosis].

I heard of lots of cures for warts: a hole of water in a rock if you come on it without looking for it; the juice of a jaggy plant that grows in sandy places called the seven brothers or the seven sisters. Other people rubbed a snail on the wart, and I heard of people getting cured of warts at St Colmcille's well in Binnion. The same well cured cows that weren't becoming *tidey* [in calf].

Paddy Óg Roddy one time had a sore under the chin that was getting worse and spreading. A travelling woman called in Roddys one day to roast a meal of potatoes for herself and noticed Paddy with his chin bandaged. She went out and gathered a handful of *crotal* [lichen] off the rocks and made a poultice of it. That one poultice left him all right. Travelling people knew a lot that way. There were more of them going around long ago with the bad times and the evictions and party trouble. A lot of them took to the roads and it was the workhouse at the rear with them.

The old people all maintained there was a cure for the evil on the seventh son. The sons had to be in a row without any daughter between them. Before my time Billy Mór of Altahall was a seventh son and the people were coming from far and near to get cured. The clergy didn't approve of it, but you'd think if the cure was born with a body there would be no harm in using it. There was a cure on the seventh daughter, too, if no sons came in between. There were seven daughters in Kerrigans and one of them, Anna Dhubh, married Paddy Mór Roddy, and they have five daughters. There was a man from Beart, named Young, who used to have cattle grazing with the Roddys and he asked Paddy what was the reason he had so many daughters. Paddy Mór said it was on the townland it was. The Roddys and the Kerrigans lived in the same townland.

If people took a pain in the pit of the stomach and it lasted for weeks, that meant the spool of the breast had fallen. It came from a hurt or if a man stressed himself. A bone or gristle below where the ribs meet in front was supposed to fall in and press on the stomach. The cure for that was to lift the spool of the breast. Paddy Doherty could do it. He put a penny on the spot and a short candle sitting on the penny. The candle was lit and a tumbler put upside down over the candle and kept close to the skin till the candle was smothered for want of air. That drew up the skin a bit into the tumbler and that helped to lift the spool of the breast from on top of the stomach.

For the heart I always heard the best thing was *dubhchosach*. This was a small fern that grew on the face of a rock. It was about as wide as your two fingers and had a thin black stem. It grows high up on the side of Bulaba on a high rock facing north. There was a chemist from Derry one time who used the *dubhchosach* and he claimed it did him good. Another plant that was good for the heart is one you get growing about old wallsteads. It grows tall with light green leaves. I heard it called the coffee plant.

The plant most used for the heart was *biolar* [watercress]. It was good for man or beast. I heard of a stirk that was poorly one time and couldn't go to the hill with the other cattle. It grazed about the river and ate a lot of wild *biolar* and soon mended up and went with the rest. Some short time after it was got drowned in a bog-hole. When they skinned and opened it up, a new heart was found growing beside the old one, about the size of a small *scoiltín* of a potato. People ate *biolar*, too, and it gave many a body a new life.

The *cradan* [burdock] root was used by people bothered with wind on the stomach. They say people with that complaint get great ease drinking the water the *cradan* root was boiled in.

The old people had a cure for the chincough [whooping cough]. The child with the chincough was put over and under a donkey three times. Two people did that, one handing the child over to the other. The donkey would get some oaten meal to eat, and the child would get a fingerful of what the donkey had left. They say there is a blessing on a donkey on account of the cross it has on its back.

I was put over and under the donkey, but I don't remember if it was any good or not. I was only two or three years at the time. The old people also gave mare's milk in bad cases of chincough. It eased the cough greatly.

Children used to take a skin disease called the *coimhthioch*. It was a kind of a rash. They got it from running about or playing over the graves of dead-born children. The cure for the *coimhthioch* was three hanks of green lint; the child was put through the hanks from right to left. There was a graveyard of that kind in Drimaneich, and one in Binnion at Ard na Ronan, one in the Isle at Pollahoota, and one at Garranarenha in Minahay.

To cure the mumps they would put a donkey's halter on the child and take him to a river that flowed between two quarter-lands and rub some of the water on his neck.

There was a cure for the decline, too, that was common in my early days. They gathered seven stalks of *sidhe* lint or fairy lint, seven stalks of the *dubhchosach*, seven more of the *bata cogaidh* [black knapweed]. These were pounded together and mixed with seven *meadars* or noggins, of water lifted from a place where three waters meet. All were heated in a cam, that's a piece of an old pot, and two spoonfuls given to the *breoiteachán* [patient] on his fast every morning for seven weeks.

There is a small plant called the *seamra Mhuire* [clover] and it was always considered lucky to carry about in your pocket. The story the old people had about it was this. There were three times that Our Lord defeated the Jews. The last time he was hunted to His own house, and He went in the front door and out the back and told the Blessed Virgin to remain inside. The chase was close behind Him and when He got outside the back door He stepped to one side and lifted a *seamra Mhuire* and held it in his hand. That made Him invisible and the Jews went rushing past Him and never saw Him. It is blessed since that time. That was the story the old women used to tell.

There was a lot of knowledgeable men in time ago with cattle and horses. Eoin O Kerrigan was a good cow-doctor and would know to look at the beast if it would get better or not. Times he wouldn't bother rising off the stool he was sitting on. That cow was done. He had some cure, they say, for the foot-and-mouth disease for he cured cattle belonging to a man in Drumfries. When Eoin came back to his own march, he wouldn't cross the brook into his own cut till they took him down other clothes to put on him. He changed there for fear he'd take the disease into his own land.

After a hard winter cattle would be very far through by the time the new grass came. They were a rickle of skin and bones. People said they were alifting. At that time of the year some heifers and stirks would get a weak back and would have to be helped up on their feet if they were lying. In my day that was called ship-tail, and the remedy was to make a small cut in the tail between the fifth and sixth joints down from the rump and tie a poultice of garlic and butter on the cut. I saw that done often. If it was a milking beast, you could taste the garlic on her milk that night.

Cattle that got at a pit of potatoes often got choked when a round potato stuck in their throat. I saw that potato broken with two small flagstones but other handy men could work it up with their two thumbs. Some cows after a heavy feed got all swelled up: their sides were up higher than their back bones. The remedy for that was stabbing. A man would put his thumb on the left hurdy [hip], and stretch his hand in the direction of the front shoulder, and where his middle finger stretched to, that was the spot. He stabbed the cow in that spot with a short knife and let out the gas. The swelling then went down. Lots of cows were cured that way, but I didn't see a cow stabbed for over thirty years. Other cow-doctors had a sort of a water gun made of a bootree [elder] stick and gave enemas with it. There was a good cow-doctor in Tullagh, and there was one time he took a whip-handle, a tether and a tether-stick out of a cow through her side, and left her as well as ever again.

Down till my father's time people went in greatly for *pisreog* cures. The old people were badly led by superstition. For bats [lumps] in calves and stirks, people used to put a lint thread round the beast's body and tie it over the back with a special knot called 'top'. If the knot ravelled out straight again that was going to be the cure. But if it got knotted and didn't run out, there was little hope for that animal.

Some cattle took a sickness and stood up all gathered up with a hump on their back and stopped chewing the cud. People said they were shot by the fairies. It was only a *tidey* cow took that ailment. The fairies were supposed to shoot the cow so as to take her milk from her when she would calve. The remedy was to burn gunpowder on the cow's back. The powder was placed in three places, on the hurdy, the small of the back and the top of the shoulder. Then the man took a piece of a burning coal in the tongs and put it under and over the cow's body three times and lit the powder each time it was crossing over the back.

For some other sickness in a cow, not chewing the cud or something, a briar that had its two ends growing in the ground was got and passed round the cow's body three times in the name of the Father and of the Son and of the Holy Ghost. Then you hit her on the stomach with your cap. Neil McEleney used to cure cattle with the briar.

I always heard you should never strike a cow with a holly stick. Holly and hazel are two trees that are gentle [enchanted]. The people used to have a rhyme 'Holly and hazel went to the wood, holly took hazel home by the lug.' That meant that holly was the master of the hazel.

Sheep used to take a disease called *galar na gcat* [cat's disease]. The ears hung down. The cure for this was to bleed the points of the ears. *Dall-amlóg* was a blindness that came over a sheep's eyes. They used to cure it by bleeding below the eyes and later on by blowing alum into the eyes with a straw.

The old people were very careful about sheep's wool. They had a box or a basket in the corner for bits of wool. If there was any lying about the floor, they were careful not to burn it. They said that was unlucky and that sheep wouldn't thrive with anybody who burned wool. I always heard, if you don't treat animals kindly, they won't do well with you.

In my grandfather's time pigs were very plentiful and litters used to graze about the hill. The year of the Dear Summer—1817—there was no sale on young pigs. A man had two litters and he dug a pit in the moss and buried them. He couldn't get a pig to thrive with him after that.

The people used to say that iron made in the forge was blessed. They never passed a piece of iron on the road without lifting it and putting it on the ditch or on a stone the way it wouldn't be lost or tramped on. The old women always put the tongs or a bar of iron over the cradle where the child was sleeping if they had to leave the house for a short while. That was against the fairies.

The old people in my young days nearly all believed in witches being able to take the milk from a neighbour's cow or the butter from a neighbour's churn. May morning was a great day for the witches. Most of the old women used to put up a maypole the evening before. They gathered a bunch of posies in the woods or about the ditches and tied it on the end of a long rod and stuck this up in the midden. They always made sure to have a piece of a whin bush along with the flowers. The maypole would be left for a day or two. None of the old people would give away a drop of milk to anybody on the May eve. Anyone looking for milk that evening would be hunted.

At calving-time the first milk had to be milked into a noggin with some silver in the bottom of it, a shilling or a half-crown. Lots of people used to rub cow-dung on a new calf's nose. All these were remedies against the witches taking away the cow's milk.

They say that before this witches were able to turn themselves into animals, hares commonly. All the old people had the story of a witch that was in this parish and no hound could take her when she turned herself into a hare. They say that Fr James Doherty put a ribbon round the hound's neck one day and the hound took her. When the hunt overtook them, they found this woman sitting under a thorn bush and her heel bleeding.

Most of the people believed in the evil eye, and you'll come across people yet. If a man had a fine thriving heifer somebody might blink her and maybe she'd fall down a ben, or get lost in a bog hole, or take some bad ailment. The person who blinked the heifer would grudge her to the man that owned her or wished him ill of her. Some people were supposed to have the power of blinking more than others, and they say people can blink without knowing they are doing it. I remember when my father long ago would be reading through the old Irish catechism and would come to the seven deadly sins, he often came out with an old saying about envy or ill-will. It was: *'Tnuth daoine chuirfeadh sé mart 'na coire, agus fear 'na cille* [The ill-will of people could send a bullock to the pot or a man to the graveyard].' That wasn't in the catechism, of course, but I wouldn't be too sure if there's not some truth in it.

The remedy against the evil eye was to tie a bit of red ribbon or thread or cloth somewhere about the animal. I remember myself at the old fair of Ballyliffin when half of the cattle there would have a bit of red yarn about them to keep the *droch shúil* [evil eye] off them.

They had strong notions, too, about things being lucky and un-lucky. They would say it wasn't lucky to sweep out the house on New Year's Day, or to meet a red-haired woman on the road, or to turn back to the house after starting out on a journey. Some of the old people were greatly led by superstitions of all kinds.

Fishermen were greatly given to superstition. My mother was telling me that in Urris, if they were turning the boat round, they always turned the nose of the boat round with the sun. The crew was always particular that no white stones were ever put into the boat for ballast; and while on the sea none of the crew would ever point at another boat with the finger but with the whole hand. Whistling was never allowed on a boat. They said, too, that the water and blood of fish that would be lying in the bottom of a boat were very powerful against the spirits of the sea. The old people could point out the *ród sidhe,* or the fairy road, where the spirits always travelled. It was three waves close together one after the other, and it was dangerous for a boat till the third wave had passed. It was the *ród sidhe* that put down an Isle of Doagh boat in 1847 when the whole crew was lost. In one of the houses that night, a hen crowed twice and someone struck her with a stick and killed her. They say that the first two crows got the boat over the first two waves of the *ród sidhe,* and that if they had let her crow the third time the boat would have survived the third wave. The women thought it was the spirits of the sea that took the men away and that they might get back. Every night for a long time they put roasted potatoes in the salt-box for the men in case they happened to get back home for a night. But whenever blood appeared on the men's old shoes, that was a sign they were gone for good.

I always heard, too, that an over-abundant crop out of all measure is a bad sign and comes before big changes. I knew a farm in the Glen where they set potatoes on a bit of bad ground, and it threw a remarkable crop. But before the next crop came off the ground, the man himself was dead, and soon after his wife died, and want and misery followed.

If three or four cows about a place were to calve and the calves to be all the same kind, all bull-calves or all cow-calves, people would take it for a bad sign. It's a thing I wouldn't like myself.

I always heard that a miss the size of a grave in a field of corn or potatoes was a sure sign of a death. I noticed it happening myself. My mother told me a relation of hers got married in Urris, and next season there was a miss in the potatoes the size of a grave with one top growing in the middle of the empty spot.

People going at the present time don't pay as much heed to signs like these as they did in times ago, but that doesn't say they are any wiser for it.

Chapter Eleven

Landlords and Tenants

AWAY BACK IN MY GRANDFATHER'S time and maybe
before it there was a great highwayman hailed from this parish, by the
name of Seán Crossach. He was a good man in ways for he robbed the
rich and gave to the poor. He had some connection with Effishmore,
and there used to be people there in my young days that were far out
connections of his.

There was one time up through this country somewhere, and Seán
Crossach was staying in a public house where a landlord's agent was
lifting rents. That night Seán lay in waiting for him and held up the
coach. He had nobody but himself, but he set up some coats and hats
and scarecrows of men behind the bushes to pretend he had a lot of
followers. When the coach stopped, he ordered his men not to fire,
and then he took all the gold and money and belongings from the
agent and made off.

Another time the soldiers were after Seán and he was hunted up
through Co. Derry till the came to the river Roe. When the chase got
tight, he jumped the river and none of the soldiers could follow him.
He sat down on the far side to rest himself, and one of the soldiers
called across to him that that was a great jump he did. Seán called
back: 'The devil thank me, I had a long enough race at it.' The people
up there called it Seán Crossach's Leap ever since. It is up about
Dungiven, and Eoin O Kerrigan saw the place when he was on his
banishment.

In the long run Seán Crossach was captured and hanged in Lifford
jail. The hanging was in public, and when he was on the scaffold he

asked if there was anybody there from Clonmany, for if there was he would leave them well off. But there was nobody there from these parts.

There was another man about that time from Minamrua. He was hanged in Edinburgh for highway robbery. They say that when he was on the scaffold, he said that when he was a child he stole spoons from a house in upper Effishmore, and if his mother had beaten him and sent him back with them that he wouldn't be there that day.

From the way the old people talked about them, I would say these men lived about 1750 or maybe before it, for my great-grandfather on my father's side settled in our present farm in 1780, and these high-waymen lived before his time. The Glen at that time belonged to a man in Beart by the name of Sweetman and he always kept a stock of cattle grazing in it. At that time it was called the Barr of Inch, but as time went on families settled down on it and broke in land. The townland of Minaduff was open to anyone who would take it at a rent of £8 a year.

After that time landlords by the name of Harvey took over the estate. Harvey built the Meentiagh Lodge sometime between the year 1817 and 1820 and held the estate till it was sold to Captain Cochrane in 1878. In Harvey's time the rent day was the twelfth of October. The agent attended at the Lodge to take in the rents and every man had to pay before twelve o'clock or he got a summons. One time it fell on the same day as the fair of the Cross, and a man from the Glen had to sell pigs at the fair to make the rent money. He sold the pigs and got on the mailcar for the rent-office but it was after twelve, and there was a summons ready for him. He had to pay 2s. extra to get it withdrawn. A man named Friel from Derry used to come to the Cross and buy live pigs and drive them to Buncrana. He'd hire carts from Clonmany with double boxing and ropes over the top and these carts would lift any pigs that would give up in the feet or couldn't make the journey. In 1891 I was in the land court and Captain Cochrane told me he was thirteen years in Meentiagh at that time.

About 1770 or so an Englishman named Charleton became land-lord of Urris. The day he arrived to see the place a big crowd of Urris men were down about Roxtown and Tullagh gathering in seaweed so he wanted some of them to go along with him to show him the extent of it. None of the men wanted to waste the day but one of them came forward and went with him. That was Niall Seán Doherty from Bun na Coille and that was how he fell in with the Charletons first. On his way back that evening he told the men who were gathering the seaweed that there would be no more of that work for him.

Charleton was a very kind-hearted man and a great gentleman. One time he went into a house in Urris and there was a *teallachan* [batch] of roasted potatoes at the side of the fire. One of the children, a girl of about seven, reached him one of the roasted potatoes. The mother scolded her for doing the like, but Charleton stood at the fireside and ate the potato and then put his hand in his pocket and gave the girl a gold sovereign and told her to buy a slip for herself.

Niall Seán's wife was from Strabane direction and she had a job as a nurse with the Charletons. Niall Seán soon became agent for them and lifted rents, and as well got the job of lifting the cuts and later became tithe-proctor. A daughter of Charleton's, who was a Mrs Merricks, became owner of the estate but she lived in England and kept Niall Seán as agent. It was from this Niall Seán Doherty that the landlords of the Glen House are descended.

I often heard of a girl of these Dohertys that she was able to go from Bun na Coille to the waterfall at the Glen House without touching the ground. She swung on the branches from one tree to another. Trees were plentiful that time, not like now.

It was in Mrs Merricks's time that Niall Seán took over part of her estate and set up as landlord at the Glen House. He and the family became tithe-proctors. The tithe money went to the support of the Protestant Church and Catholics had to pay it too. The Waterloo priest spent three months in Lifford jail for refusing to pay it, and when he was released the people turned up out of face to meet him.

He made a speech out at the Glen House and he said the day would come when there wouldn't be seed, breed or generation of the Glen House people in this parish.

The old people always said that Niall Seán had great influence with the authorities. During the wars of Napoleon he would save any man from being pressed into the navy on payment of a guinea. Many a guinea he got that time, and he was even lifting guineas for days after the war was over in 1815 till the people got to know.

Niall Seán had three sons, Michael Mór, Denis and Owen, and one daughter who married Barney Farren, and another who married Doherty of Whitecastle, and that was how the Glen House people were connected with the Cochranes.

Owen married Fr Shiels's niece and got Termain with her and they had one son, William.

Denis lived in Keelogs and was landlord of Tirhoran.

Michael Mór, the other son of Niall Seán, got the Glen House. He got married to a woman from Derry who was a Protestant. The agreement they had was that the sons would be reared Catholic and the daughters Protestant. That was carried out. Michael Mór had four sons and three daughters. The sons were Michael Óg, James Walker, Andrew and Edward.

The sons were all baptised by the priest and went to Mass with the father and had a front seat in the chapel.

One of the daughters married Dr Irwin, a very upright, reasonable man and a good doctor. Another daughter married the Rev. Young, the rector. Mr Young was a very good man and the people had a great word on him. He was from Co. Down. He had great influence. A line from him would nearly take a man from the gallows. I know myself he saved two men from transportation for waylaying a bailiff.

One Sunday a difference arose between Michael Mór and Fr O Donnell, the Waterloo priest, over a collection at the chapel gate. It ended up that Michael turned home and took the sons with him and never went to the chapel after. That was how the Glen House Dohertys became Protestants.

A lot of old people blamed Fr O Donnell a great deal for he was a very hot-tempered man. They say Michael Mór was a man always paid his dues well. Up to the time of this row the priests often went out to the old graveyard at the Protestant church to officiate at funerals, for lots of people kept on burying there after the new graveyard was opened. But after this row with the Glen House people, none of the priests ever went out to the old graveyard. The priest would bless the clay and read the prayers over the corpse at the chapel, and someone else at the funeral would throw the clay over the coffin. The last Catholic to be buried in the old graveyard was an old woman by the name of McDermott. She had been evicted and died in the workhouse. That was in 1880.

James Walker Doherty became a solicitor, and died the year before I was born. Andrew was a boy in Derry at school when he took bad and died there. Michael Óg lived about the Glen House till he died there. Edward, the last of them, managed the affairs of the Glen House till he died and then the land was divided among the tenants.

In Binnion after McNeill's time, the place was taken over by a man named Buchanan. He was landlord of the estate and grazed a lot of cattle. He shipped cattle and geese. There's a fence built up through Meendoran from the river to the lough. It was built in his time and is still called Buchanan's Ditch. It goes zig-zagging up the brae-face so that the cattle would get shelter no matter what airt the wind was blowing from.

When Buchanan came here on his first visit, he saw people going through his cornfields and told his foreman or steward to get his gun. The foreman told him the people were in great want and that they were only pulling the *praiseach* [charlock] to make soup and that they had little else to eat. It must have been a year of famine, and would be around 1770 or 1780. When Buchanan saw the poverty of the people, he landed a sloop of oaten meal at Suil rock and divided it out where it was needed.

As Buchanan and his wife would be passing through Moville on their way to and from England, Mrs Buchanan fell in with a young lad in Moville by the name of Michael Loughrey. The Loughreys had a public house or hotel on the main street. She took a great fancy to him and brought him with her to England. Some time later a son of Mrs Buchanan's died in India, and Michael went out and took the corpse home to be buried. He used to manage all their affairs for them, and when they got old, they offered him two quarterlands they had in Binnion and another in Cabry. Michael Loughrey bought them and came to live in Binnion. That was about the year 1814.

The present house in Binnion was built in 1816. When the building was going on, Michael had a ganger from Co. Derry quarrying stones. Whatever quarry the men were sent to, they thought it was gentle and refused to lift a sledge. So the ganger took off a red scarf he had round his neck, tied a knot on it and threw it on top of the rock. He told the men to be back next morning and that they'd see if it was gentle or not. Next morning the scarf was the same way as it was left the day before, so the men fell to the sledging, and there was no more word of the fairies. A part of the house goes back to the time of McNeill and maybe before that. I heard there used to be a monastery there in times ago, but I never heard anything about it.

Chapter Twelve

Factions

IN MY GRANDFATHER'S TIME AND down to my father's time there were party-men of all kinds and lots of people got into bother over the head of them. I heard of one of the Lynchs at Drumfries who was transported over some party bother and was never heard of again. About the year 1800 Micky Roddy's granduncle, Hughie, was on his banishment and there was a warrant out for his arrest. Hughie was hidden in an old cave above the house at the foot of Bulaba. It was used as a malt-house in the days of the poteen. The heather grew down over it and you would pass it by unknownst. I was often in it myself.

One night Hughie went down by the house for something to eat likely, but as he went nearer, the geese started gragging, and he knew there was something wrong. What was it but the yeomen had the house surrounded. He went back and hid in the malt-house. When the yeomen couldn't find Hughie, they lifted Oweny who was only a young lad of twelve out of his bed and took him with them back to Malin. The journey of fourteen miles in the dead of the night was more than Oweny was able for and he gave up on the way and one of the soldiers carried him on his shoulders. The soldier told Oweny he could have taken his brother Hughie if he wanted to because he saw him the time the geese gragged. They got no information out of Oweny, and he was let out next day. A grandson of Hughie's was afterwards editor of the *Derry Journal*.

The country was in a bad way with parties of different kinds. People were waylaid along the roads at night and what-not. Drink was cheap and that made things worse. Fr Matthew made a round of the country, and held great meetings, giving the people the pledge. He was always well published beforehand. The pledge he gave was a life-pledge against drink, except when the doctor allowed it. Parish priests had power to give the Fr Matthew pledge and medal. At that time all the people in the Glen took the pledge and got a medal, but the only two that carried it out were Eoin O Breslin and Neddy McEleney. And if they did itself, it was for their own safety, for they attended fairs and markets and wanted to have daylight home with them.

One tenth of October fair of Ballyliffin Eoin and his brother Neal were coming home. Eoin thought it might be dangerous coming down the chapel glen and he cut up over Cleagh hill. Neal went round the road and there was a set of men in front of him. They mistook him for Eoin and fell to him with the sticks and he got a bad beating and a young son who was with him got such abuse that he was lame for life.

Roger Roddy, a brother of Hughie's, died as the result of a beating he got at the fair of Ballyliffin. Cheap drink was the cause of a lot of this trouble. Sure drink was for next to nothing, tenpence a pint maybe.

Another strong party-man was Neal Roe Doherty. He was a son of George Doherty and had a brother a priest, Fr Edward Doherty. The priests were out strong against the parties, and one Sunday, Fr O'Donnell, the Waterloo priest, was preaching against them when Neal Roe went up on the altar and got him by the throat and bent him back over the altar. Oh, I believe that was a big day in the chapel. It was a day the old people never forgot. None of them liked to speak about it. That was the highest day Neal Roe ever saw. There's not one belonging to him in the parish today.

There was a bad end on the party-men, in particular on the headsmen. They all fell to poverty and wretchedness after it.

The headsmen all had a book for swearing the members in. There was a man in Rooskey by the name of Donaghey and he was a leader of the Wright's Men. A son of his, Charlie, went to Latin school in Co. Derry and went on for the church but wouldn't get on for this diocese and went to America and was ordained there. He lived no time. He got a short life.

The time of the parties no man with money about him was safe going the roads after night. Jimmy Barr went up to the June fair in Derry one time with seventeen head of *tidey* heifers. When he sold them he set out for home but night overtook him in Buncrana. Coming out past Cock Hill he heard steps coming after him. He knew it was some gang that knew he was coming from the fair and would be likely to have money on him. So he sharpened his step and kept ahead of them. When he reached Drumfries he decided to go into Dohertys but everybody was in bed. There was a cart on the street with the shafts on the ground. So Jimmy got under the cart and hid. Soon the footsteps came his length. There were eight or ten of them in it and them saying to the others: 'If he's the devil himself, we'll overtake him before he's at Carraicalough.' Jimmy let them past and then cut up over the hill past Minamala and got home that way.

Jimmy was a well-to-do man that married late in life but the money soon ran done. His wife used to say, 'Bachelor's money isn't lucky.'

Chapter Thirteen

Education

IN MY FATHER'S TIME AND BEFORE it there was always some kind of a school kept going in Meentiagh Glen. It would be held in a barn or some *cró* of a house with stones round the wall for seats. The last of the old teachers was a man by the name of Graham. He was a well educated man and a poet but he was greatly given to the drink. I don't know where Graham went to or what happened to him. He was a good teacher and turned out better scholars than what's going now.

Everybody attending Graham's school spoke Irish and knew nothing else. But he taught English and figuring. When they were learning the English letters they picked them up from the names of things that had the same shape as the letters:

A—*cúpla toighe,* B—*spéaclóirí,* C—*déanamh na gealaighe,* D—*bogha is saighead,* E—*áit toighe,* F—*cos speile,* G—*crudh gearrain,* H—*geafta,* I—*bata,* J—*camán,* K—*eochair an dorais,* L—*súiste,* M—*scoil oidhche,* N—*lena chois sin,* O—*gealach,* P—*cor shúgán,* Q—*réalt an rubaill,* R—*ruball an mhadaidh,* S—*an t-eascon,* T—*cos spáid,* U—*crudh asail,* V—*compáis,* W—*gearran gorm,* X—*an Croch cheasta,* Y—*cos an raca,* Z—*crúca.*

[A—the couple of a house, B—spectacles, C—the shape of the moon, D—a bow and arrow, E—the foundation of a house, F—the handle of a scythe, G—a horseshoe, H—a gate, I—a stick, J—a caman, K—the key of a door, L—a flail, M—night-

school, N—beside it, O—the moon, P—a throw-hook, Q—a comet, R—dog's tail, S—the eel, T—a spade-handle, U—a donkey shoe, V—a compass, W—a dark grey horse, X—the Crucifix, Y—the handle of a rake, Z—a crook.]

It was all slates they used till they got on a distance and then they wrote with quill pens. The teacher would have a bunch of feathers and trimmed them himself as they were needed. They made some sort of ink, as far as I remember hearing, from the seeds of the elder tree.

My father spent a while with Graham but went later on to a school run by William McLaughlin. He learned to read English there but he picked up the Irish reading himself when he got used to the Irish type. A neighbour of ours at the same school learned to measure land well. That was Micky the Man. He could measure a field that was a round circle. Very few could do that.

Graham was a great poet, too, and all the old people had songs that Graham composed. He used to spend a lot of his time about Carn on tears of drink and lodged at a public house run by a man called Neil Gill. Graham made a song about the house and people. It was called 'Neil Gill's Inishowen' and I heard my father singing it that often that I remember it yet:

Ye lads of true merit, of candour and spirit,
Who like to be jolly if you have got time,
Draw nigh to the table and drink while you're able,
I'll sing you a song so give ear to my rhyme.
I mean not to wrangle, dispute, nor to jangle,
To each jolly toper I mean to make known,
The sweet animation of dear distillation,
Called by its title Neil Gill's Inishowen.

As whiskey's my theme, you critics don't blame me,
If I'm incorrect from the fumes of the grog,

My muse has elated and intoxicated,
A while on Pegasus our poesy to jog.
The Mount of Parnassus or wings of Pegasus,
Or Halcyon's waters I freely disown.
There's a fountain that's purer I'm certainly surer
Called by its title Neil Gill's Inishowen.

You lawyers who toil o'er the midnight oil,
In support of your clients their cause to maintain,
You'll enquire and read and slowly proceed,
And of the bank notes their pocket books drain.
When you go to the Bar to commence verbal war,
Amongst all your tribe it is very well known,
You will open your throat and read out the notes,
If you get but one glassful of Gill's Inishowen.

You desponding lovers who are seldom or never
But sighing and sobbing, very often in vain,
Lay over your folly, your sad melancholy,
And take my advice the sly wench to obtain.
Regard not her flaring but while she's endearing
Or blinding your armour with whiskey along,
Give her a glass often, there's nothing can soften
The heart of a fair maid, like Gill's Inishowen.

You whiskey retailers that are subject to failures,
I mean you corruptors of Branney's poteen,
You may come to Carn a lesson to learn,
For Gill can instruct you, you know what I mean.
Likewise you distillers, you maltsters and millers,
Who toast a good health to King George on the throne,
Come join us in chorus we'll drink what's before us,
And toast a good health to Neil Gill's Inishowen.

You men of the college how great is your knowledge,
Pray who understands the Creator like you?
You actors and teachers and likewise you preachers,
A word in your ear I mean to construe.
While you're converting apostate dissenters,
Or preaching the scripture to laymen unknown
I know no quotation could cherish oration,
As well as a bumper of Gill's Inishowen.

This famous enholder of whom I have told you,
In a village called Carn retails a good drop,
Who merits applauding being wide of defrauding,
And kind to all strangers that call at his shop.
His wife I'll commend her, no soothing pretender,
Who pockets no profit but what is her own.
She is always delighted to help the benighted
With good entertainment of Gill's Inishowen.

My father could sing it well when he had a drop taken. I never heard what became of Graham but William McLaughlin came after him sometime around 1820 before the national schools were heard of. It was only English songs that Graham made.

As well as the sort of schools that men like Graham ran, there was always a Latin school in Clonmany till the time St Columb's College was opened. The earliest Latin teacher I heard of was by the name of McColga and he put three bishops through his hands. Dr O Doherty, Dr Kelly and Dr Maginn. After his time a Master Kane ran a Latin school at the Cross. He wasn't a native of the parish. The last Latin teacher was Jimmy Doherty of Tirhoran. He was educated in Maynooth College, but his health gave up. Jimmy Doherty, to look at, would pass for a full *cluasán*, but in place of that he was a very clever man.

At Jimmy Doherty's Latin school there used to be up to thirty students at the one time. They stopped in houses round about unless a house that had young children. They'd have no way for them. I remember students by the name of Lafferty and Doherty of Gleneely and another named Mooney from Culdaff. But they were from all parts. Jimmy used to teach the Latin while he would be out in the fields setting a ridge of potatoes, or ploughing, or whatever else would be on. The students would be about the head or foot of the fields, or some of them walking alongside him.

A professor from Dublin called in Tirhoran to see Jimmy one day in the dead of summer. He had met some of Jimmy's students, and they were such good Latin scholars that he wanted to see the man that taught them. This day Jimmy was out weeding potatoes. He never kept himself too tidy at any time, so when the professor called, the ones in the house got his good suit out the back window of the room and up to the field to Jimmy. He changed in the field and came down then and spent the evening chatting with the professor.

In my father's young days, the old master, William McLaughlin, came here from Iskaheen along with his mother.

He was a man that was fond of the drink. He could drink a pint and it wouldn't seize on him. He ran a kind of a school in the Glen and when the national schools came out he was appointed to Drumfries. He told me himself his first year's salary was £16. He would have made more gathering rags.

One of the O Donnell girls of Rushfield ran away with him. Her people were mad against the match and didn't speak of either of them for long enough. She was a niece of Fr O Donnell, the Waterloo priest. After some time she got to teach along with him at a salary of £8 a year.

He was an educated man and a smart man and a great speaker on stage or platform. The family was smart, too, but they were all fond of the drink. I remember one of them called Oweny and he could turn himself over like a showman and jump out and into six barrels in a row. I saw him afterwards when he came from America and he was as stiff as a crowbar. One of the sons, Charley, got the school when the old master died. There's not one of the name left now.

Chapter Fourteen

The Exploits of Eoin O Kerrigan

ANOTHER BREED OF PEOPLE WHO came from Iskaheen or the Foreside was the Kerrigans. They came here about 1780, the mother and four sons. Two of these went abroad and the other two, Donal and Felimy, settled in the Glen. The mother took them from the Foreside for fear they would take up with the trading vessels along the Foyle.

Donal got married to a woman named McEleney from Meendoran. They were married by Fr Corr on the roadside at Meendoran Bridge. That was before there was any chapel here for it wasn't built till Fr Shiels's time in 1795. Donal had a great clutch of a family. There was Sorcha, Roise, Caitriona, Nuala, Brighid, Eibhlin, Maire Mhór, Anna Dhubh and two sons, Eoin and Felimy.

Eoin was an outstanding man. If his whole career was written down it would be great reading. He was born in 1805, five years before my father, and settled down in the present place in 1840 when the land was up. In the year of 1835 a couple of tithe-viewers came up from Clonmany, tithe-viewing for Rev. Dobbs. It happened to be the early morning of Eoin O Breslin's wedding day and the people were all going home after the wedding when word went round that the tithe-men were in the Glen. Eoin O Kerrigan and a crowd gathered and threw the two of them into a dam called Poll an Duibheagain and gave them bad abuse. This dam was a kind of a bottomless hole in the meadows. The men begged to be let away with their life. So Neily Barr from Bavil got the loan of Jamesy Barr's prayer book and put the tithe-men on their oath that they'd never come back on the same mission. Neily was for handing the book to the men but Eoin O Kerrigan told him to throw it on the ground and make them lift it.

Jamesy was a very religious man who devoted his life to reading and praying and always carried a holy book about with him.

When the tithe-men reached home, they swore an information on the men that attacked them and a warrant was issued for their arrest. Eoin took to the hills and disappeared and didn't come back for three years till all blew over. He had his trade as a cow-doctor when he returned. But Neily Barr and Jamesy were lifted and they got a year apiece in Lifford jail. While they were there they had a bad time with dirt and vermin of all kinds. So Jamesy wrote to a man called Templemore in Inch and complained to him about what they had to put up with. Templemore must have been a landlord or a man of great influence for he sent word to the headsmen of the jail that if his two tenants weren't treated right, he would see more about it. They got better treatment from that on but they had to put in their full time.

The Glen was never levied for tithe after that. Some people say that the whole Glen should belong to Clonmany parish by right. When the railway was being built in 1900, the sappers told me that the river between Owenbwee and Carrohill was a parish boundary and that the Minamala river was the boundary on the other side.

While Eoin was on his banishment, he tramped through all Donegal and Derry and Tyrone and further. He would stop at some house for a while and then move on. There were few people or places he didn't know about. He said he never called at any house unless some place that had a good midden. That was a sign they had plenty of milk in that house. He could tell stories about Jack's Fair, and Milford, and Letterkenny, and Dungiven, and Sligo and where-not.

He was a clever man. He said himself that the only person who ever got the better of him was a Sligo woman. He called at a certain house for lodging where a woman lived alone. She said she wouldn't put him up unless he could beat her at three standing jumps. Eoin agreed. She stood at the back wall, and cut three jumps, and just reached the doorstep. Eoin tried next, and his third jump took him out a couple of feet beyond the door. Then she slammed the door, and bolted it, and left him out.

After he came back home and settled down, he was in great demand as a cow-doctor and was a very knowledgeable man with all classes of animals. He went across to Scotland often and took back horses from the Highlands and went round all the fairs selling them. He took across Scotch sheep, too, for they were coming in greatly at that time. He would be away in Scotland for weeks at a time, trogging in sheep and lambs and geese and things. One time he was driving a flock of geese through the Highlands somewhere and he met a woman. She said 'Good luck to your six score geese.' It was six score he had with him, and he often wondered how she knew the number by looking at them.

Eoin was a well built man and had the strength of two men in his arms and shoulders. He could handle a stick well, too. There were few could handle a stick as well, and few men would take his on.

A neighbour of his, Jimmy Doherty, often went along with Eoin to Scotland and round the fairs. One night they were crossing on the boat and a storm came on, and everyone thought all hands were going to the bottom. Eoin and Jimmy held a consultation about the state of their souls but there was no priest on board to make their confession to. So Eoin told Jimmy he always heard that in a case of necessity it would do to make your confession to a lay-body when there was no priest to be had. And so they agreed they would hear one another's confession. Eoin first got Jimmy to go down on his knees and make his confession. But when it came Eoin's turn, he looked round at the sky and said he thought it was fairing up a bit and that he'd wait a while. So Eoin got out of making his confession altogether.

In 1887 there was a mission in Clonmany run by three Redemptorist fathers, Fr Graham and Fr O'Brian and Fr Doherty. Eoin made the mission and I'm told that the fathers warned him that he was as lawfully bound to keep Jimmy's confession secret just as much as the priest was. Later there was a station in Kerrigans and when the confessions were all heard, Fr Blaney came up from the room with Paddy Óg Roddy, the last man to be heard. Fr Blaney stood with his back to the fire and asked Eoin was it true that he heard a man's confession one time. Eoin said it was true enough. Fr Blaney then asked Eoin what did the man tell him. Eoin said he'd tell him that whenever Fr Blaney would tell him what Paddy Óg Roddy confessed. Fr Blaney laughed and said he couldn't do that. Eoin then said that what Jimmy told him in confession he kept to himself and never breathed a word of it to any human being.

In Eoin's young days the Harveys were in Meentiagh Lodge and had a big monkey for a pet. Eoin used to be employed at times about the Lodge. One day they were all going away and Eoin was left to attend to the monkey. At dinner-time Eoin took a dish of beef and bread to the room where the monkey was kept. Instead of taking the dinner the monkey made for Eoin and would have made bad work of him only that Eoin always carried a stick. With a blow of the stick about the head Eoin killed the monkey. Then he took a bone out of the dish and stuck it well back in the monkey's throat and left it lying there. When the Harveys returned, there was a whole enquiry until Eoin showed them the bone and told them the monkey had choked himself. There was great grieving over that same monkey. The Harveys got a coffin made for him and held a funeral service and buried him in the garden.

One evening Eoin was coming from Derry with a horse and cart. Micky Bhriney Doherty was along with him. Coming through Buncrana they fell in with the old master, William McLaughlin. He asked Eoin to take home a two-hundred-weight bag of meal for him in the cart. On the way home William and Micky walked on in front and William produced a bottle and they finished it between them. When Eoin got their length and got the smell of the drink on them, he went mad altogether and stopped the horse and threw off the meal on the roadside. The old master had to get it on his back and carry it the rest of the way.

Eoin died at Candlemas 1895. At the funeral Fr Blaney spoke of the way he stood up for his faith, not only at home but across the water. There never will be a man again the like of Eoin O Kerrigan.

Chapter Fifteen

The Famine

MY FATHER AND MOTHER OFTEN spoke about the time of the Famine when the rot came on the potatoes in 1845. The first failure of the potatoes came in that year, and the next year was the *bliain na scidín* [the year of the small potatoes]. The year of 1847 was the year the relief came when the Free Trade Bill was passed and the Indian meal came into the country first. Relief works were started and the *brachán* [stirabout] was given out in every parish. People came with their cans, and the *brachán* was made in a boiler and they took home canfuls. The relief wasn't a free grant from the government: it all had to come off the cuts later on.

As far as I could make out, this parish came off better than lots of places.

I often heard that the Dear Summer of 1817 was a worse famine in many ways than the Famine of 1847. In 1847 meal went to 10s. a peck. A peck of meal was 10 lbs weight. I heard of Oweny Mhichíl that he sold a springing heifer in Carn and on his way home he bought the worth of the heifer of meal in Shiels's at the Cross and carried the meal on his back to Effishmore. A young heifer at that time would go maybe between twenty-five and thirty shillings.

The women pulled *praiseach* [charlock] round the fields and made it into a kind of broth with turnips or whatever else they could get. There was a lot of travelling people on the roads, coming from places where the Famine was worse. I heard of a travelling man being found dead along the road and his mouth full of grass and weeds. One day at dinner-time a man and a boy called at a house in Gortnahinson and asked them for God's sake to give them the skins of the potatoes in the basket. They made balls of the skins and ate them and moved on up the Owenirk road. Some days after that the boy was found dead on the old road below Minamrua.

I heard, too, that in 1846 Johnny Bán Doherty's father dug in his field of potatoes for two days before he got as many potatoes as made the poundies for Halloweve night.

In some places the times were so bad that people couldn't hold on to their bits of land and farms were going for next to nothing. Porters' farm in Ballinlough went from £17 and sure the same place was sold here lately for £500. I knew another farm to be bought in the bad times for a hundredweight of meal, and changed hands again for £3.

Chapter Sixteen

Pastimes

WHEN I WAS GROWING UP, PEOPLE hadn't as easy a way of living on them as they have now. There was little word of schooling or things like that. We had to help with the work in the spring-time, and foot turf, and go after sheep, or help at the harvest according to the season. It was a common thing for youngsters of six and seven years to be hired out as herds from May to Holiday [21 November], and they never saw the inside of a school, unless maybe an odd while of a winter. I spent only two or three winters at school myself. I picked up a bit of reading and was getting on to figuring a little but I never got as far as the second book. The only ones to get any chance that time were the younger members of a family.

The books we had were at half price. The government paid the other half. There was no Irish allowed, though the scholars could all speak it and the old master too. It is a great change to see the Irish in all the schools for the first time, but the young people going now can't get a way with it right. The language will never die out and that is a good thing. There was little *meas* [respect] on Irish in my time. If you didn't know a bit of English you got nowhere.

For writing we used quill pens and then the ordinary pens, or we wrote on slates with slate pencils. They are done away with now.

During the summer-time we were hardly ever at school. We were kept home for herding mostly, keeping cows from breaking over the march into a neighbour's field, or trying to keep them grazing round the edge of a field that corn or potatoes were growing in. It was nice in the good weather. When it came on wet, you had to be out just the same with a bag across your shoulders. I used to shove one corner into the other and make a hood for my head and let the rest of the bag hang down round me. My mother had a stock of good linen sacks with her from Urris and they made good wear for a wet day.

If two or three of us were herding nearby we would be at some pastime but we couldn't take our eyes off the cows for some of them were very cute. The commonest game we had was a game called 'duck'. A fair-sized stone with a flat top was set up. It was called the 'granny'. Each of us had a round *duirling* of a stone, called the 'duck', for throwing, and whoever got nearest the granny put his duck on top of it. We would all throw then and try to knock the duck off, and then run to get our own duck on its place. Duck was a handy game for we could play it on any kind of ground and there was no want of stones.

A great pastime we had, too, when herding, was plaiting rushes into the shape of a whip-handle called a bugaboo, or making rush hats. These were shaped like a dunce's cap and went up into a point. We had leggings, too, the same way.

If we were herding about the woods we made bows and arrows out of sally rods and shot at birds, mostly crows and magpies. Sometimes we put up a cockshot, a stone or a turf, but we hardly ever hit anything. In the spring when the sap would be rising in the bushes every young fellow made a whistle or two for himself out of a branch of the rowan tree. We cut a straight piece without knots and tapped the bark round and round with the handle of a knife or a stick until the bark got loose and came off in a piece. Then we cut a bit for a mouthpiece with a groove along the top of it and cut a hole in the bark behind the mouthpiece and stopped up the other end. Some would put a pea inside the whistle. You could hear it half-a-mile away. They soon got broken up in our pocket but it wasn't hard to make another.

The spring was a great time for birds' nests. Whoever got a nest first claimed it. We never thought it any harm to rob the nests of magpies or crows for they lifted eggs and young chickens. Nobody would touch a robin's nest. The robin was supposed to be a holy bird and the old people said it cursed anybody that robbed its nest. The robin's curse was:

Má's duine beag a rois mo nead,
Go dtabairidh Dia chiall do;
Ma's duine mór a rois mo nead,
Go gcuiridh Sé faoi chlár é.

[*If it is a young person who robs my nest,*
May God give him sense;
But if it's a grown person who robs my nest,
My God put him in a coffin.]

They used to say, if you lifted an egg every day from the wren's nest, that she would keep on laying till she would kill herself. But from experience, if you handle the eggs or nest of any bird a time or two, the bird can smell your hand and will forsake the nest.

In the spring-time everyone was on the look-out for the cuckoo. She always had a smaller bird along with her. It was unlucky to hear the first cuckoo in spring on a fasting stomach, the old people said, or to see a snail on a stone or a young foal with its rump to you. This was the rhyme they had:

Chonnaic mé an searrach lena chúl liom.
Chuala mé an chuach gan greim in mo bhroinn.
Chonnaic mé seilide ar an leac shleamhnain lom.
Agus b'fhusa domh a shílstin nach n-eireódh an bhliain seo liom.

[*I saw a foal, with its back to me.*
I heard the cuckoo without a bite in my stomach.
I saw a snail on the bare slippery flag.
And it was easy for me to see that the year wouldn't be a success.]

The cuckoo always took a storm with her, and I never remember a year yet that the cuckoo-storm didn't come a few weeks after Branney's days [the first three days of April].

There was no eagles in my time though I heard of a man who saw an eagle in Glassmullan hill near Doo Lough. It lifted a *whitterit* [stoat] and both of them fought it out in the air over the man's head, and at the rear the eagle fell to the ground with its throat cut. The *whitterit* is very wicked and hard to kill. Cats are hard to kill too. Tomás Carey of Owenbwee caught a live fox on Sliabh Sneachta one time and put it in a barrel to take it to Derry next day. There was an old useless cat about the house that he wanted rid of and he put her into the barrel along with the fox. In the morning the fox was dead and the cat jumped out when they lifted the lid.

We hunted rabbits and hares with dogs. Every young fellow wanted to have a dog that could run well. We called the dogs names like Collie, Randy, Price, Gip, or Fly. I had a dog one time and I called him Tullairt because when he was a pup he was like a ball of wool.

On Sundays in the summer-time all the boys of an age in the townland went up the brook fishing. We fished with our hands. We started up high near the foot of Bulaba and dug sods and stopped up the river. Then we went down and fished the holes out of face. The water could be low and we caught the trout with our hands. We baled out water sometimes but most of the water drained away as long as the sods held back the flow. It was a pastime I liked well. I knew every hole in the brook and nearly every stone that a trout or eel could hide under.

We often fished with a bag-net as well. We put a bent rod in the mouth of the bag to keep it open and set the bag at a narrow neck of water. Then we went into the hole with sticks and prodded the banks and stones to chase the trout into the bag-net. We often caught six or maybe a dozen that way. We were always on the bare feet in my early days. We hadn't a shoe to our feet till we were nearly man big.

Pitching buttons was a great game with us. We often cut the buttons off our clothes to play with. That led to great rows in the house many a time.

We used to make water guns out of a bootree stick. The inside is soft and can be cleaned out. Then we got a thin stick and tied a piece of cloth on the end of it so that it fitted the hole well. At the knot we made a small hole to take in the water. We could suck up the full of it of water and shoot it out again, and young people had great fun with it.

Any dolls I saw were home-made ones out of pieces of cloth. But a handy carpenter could make a wooden man with jointed legs and arms. He danced on a board when you held him over it and hit the board.

Children were easily pleased at that time besides what they are now. When my mother was at the fair of Ballyliffin, or the gooseberry fair, or the apple fair in Buncrana, we would all be down about the rocks watching out for her coming home. When she came home she always said: '*An t'é is feárr a bhéas liom, 'sé feárr a gheobhas roinn* [Whoever I like best gets the best share].' She would have gooseberries or apples or sweets with her, and maybe a length of ribbon for my sister Síle. We would gather round then and everything would be divided.

Another saying I heard with my mother was '*Fhad is a bhéas an mhéar ag sileadh bíonn an teanga ag moladh* [While the hand is giving the tongue is praising].' That was said about people who were getting the loan of things like milk or meal or that. While they were getting, they would be very civil, the tongue would be praising.

In time of snow a great game the young people had was catching birds under a basket. I often caught them that way. I propped up a basket with a piece of a stick and tied a long thread to the stick. I put oaten meal under the basket and hid in the barn or in the byre and held the end of the thread. Birds came round to get the meal, and I gave the thread a pull, and the basket fell down, and they were caught that way. We let them go again mostly. But sometimes we cooked the pigeons and blackbirds and ate them.

About the fireside young people passed the time scoring with the shank of a clay pipe on the flagstone. That was the way I learned my figures and a lot of the letters. There was nothing going but clay pipes that time. A man buying a bag of meal got an ounce of tobacco and a clay pipe thrown in for nothing. There were no such things as cigarettes heard tell of. Pipe-smoking was a common thing with the women as well as the men in my early days. Taking the whole side of the Glen from Devlins to Roddys all the women on that run smoked the clay pipe, except for two, Ann Roddy and my mother. The clay pipes and things like that were kept in the bowils in the backstone.

Sitting about the fire at night the children used to light fir-splits and put them round and round like a wheel to see who could keep the red point the longest. They had a rhyme to say called *Roithlean rotha* but I forget it. Round the fire they played a game called *Lurapog a larapog*, counting round on their toes till the rhyme would end and whoever the last word fell on got a tap with the rod. A house with young children was a noisy place many a time, our own as well as the rest. But it's a long while now since the music of children was heard in this house. It'll be eighty years and more.

It was sitting about the fire that we learned our prayers and old rhymes and things. As well as the prayers for the Rosary the old people had prayers of their own, the old women mostly, when they would be putting on their clothes, or lighting the fire, or going a journey, or leaving the chapel on a Sunday after Mass:

Beannacht leat, a Mhuire,
Beannacht leat, a Chríost,
Go gcumhdaighidh sibh m'anam,
Go bpillidh mé arís.

[*Goodbye, Mary,*
Goodbye, Christ,
Guard my soul,
Till I return again.]

When they would be going to bed they said a prayer:

Luighimse le Dia,
Go luighidh Dia liom.
Sciath Mhuire ag mo cheann,
Dídean Mhuire fá mo dhá bhonn,
Crios Mhuire tharam.
Muire is a Mac, Brighid is a brat, Pádraig na bhFeart,
Idir muid-inne agus an t-olc, a Thighearna, Amen.

[*I lie down with God.*
May God lie down with me.
Mary's shield at my head,
Mary's mantle around my feet,
Mary's girdle about me.
Mary and her Son, Brigid and her cloak, Patrick of the miracles,
All stand between us and evil, Amen.]

When anybody would be in great pain there was a prayer they had
to ease the pain:

A Mhuire Mhór, máthair an Rí,
Déan mo shaodhsa le do Mhac,
A ghnúis is gile ná an ghrian,
Nach bhfulaingidh 'mo phian-sa i bhfad.

[*O Mary, mother of the King,*
Make my request to your Son,

Whose countenance is brighter than the sun,
That my pain may not last long.]

When the child in the cradle would take a hiccough my mother would say '*Snag bhisigh ort, a thaiscidh* [You have the hiccough of improvement, my treasure].' A hiccough was said to be a sign of thriving. When the children would be going to bed the others in the house would say '*Luigh slán is éirigh follain* [Sleep well and rise healthy.]'

Around the fireside we picked up rhymes of all kinds:

Seacht scadán sáith an bhradáin;
Seacht rón sáith na muice mara;
Seacht muc mara sáith an tsliogaire;
Seacht sliogair sáith an tsiorc.

[*Seven herrings is enough for the salmon;*
Seven seals is enough for the porpoise;
Seven porpoises is enough for the dolphin;
Seven dolphins is enough for the shark.]

Another rhyme we were fond of saying was:

Tá mise ag dul ag iarraidh madaidh;
Madadh a ruaigfeadh cat;
Cat a lighfeadh im;
Im a chuirfidhe ar chosa gadhair;
Gadhar a shmámhfadh uisce;
Uisce a chuirfidhe ar chloich;
Cloch a chuimleochaidhe ar thuaigh;
Tuagh a ghearrfadh slat;
Slat a ruaidhfeadh 'na masaí ag na buic
Atá ag déanamh milleadh mire ar an tír.

[*I am looking for a dog;*
A dog that would chase a cat;
A cat that would lick butter;
Butter you would put on a hound's feet;
A hound to swim across water;
Water to put on a stone;
A stone to rub on a hatchet;
A hatchet to cut a rod;
And a rod to switch the ruffians
That are destroying the country.]

In the old houses before this crickets were a common thing about the backstone. You could hardly hear your ears with them. We used to throw bits of tallow or bread beside the holes they came out of. One would help the other to pull it in if the piece was too heavy. We never killed any crickets. They were gentle. I always heard, if a person killed a cricket, all the others would gather and eat holes in his clothes and cut his socks.

Cats sometimes ate crickets, but the cat that did that never thrived and was always starved looking. The people used to say about anybody that was ill-thriven that he was like a cat would be eating crickets.

Chapter Seventeen

Set Nights

ON SET NIGHTS WE HAD FUN OF different kinds in the house. The set nights were Halloweve, Christmas Eve and St Brigid's Eve. On set nights such as these we always had a supper of poundies and butter. Before the supper started my father said the grace before meals:

Bail na gcúig n-arán is an dá iasc
Ar an chúig mhíle do rann Dia.
Rath ó'n Rí a rinne an rann,
Go dtige sé ar ár gcuid is ar ár gcrann.
A Thiarna is tú a cheannaigh mé,
Beannaigh mé féin, mo chuid, is mo chuideachta.

[*The blessing of the five loaves and the two fishes*
That God divided on the five thousand.
With a blessing from the King who made the divide,
May it come on our food and on our lot.
O Lord, you who have redeemed me,
Bless myself, my meal and my company.]

It was only on set nights that I heard him giving out this prayer.

Most nights the time was passed listening to the old people telling stories about Fionn Mac Cumhaill and Oisin and the Fianna, and Cuchulainn and Conor and Fergus, and stories of giants and witches and fairies and what-not. Some of these stories were so long that they wouldn't be finished at bedtime, so the old man would carry on the next night where he left off.

My father was a good story-teller, and so was Micky the Man, and Anna Dhubh, and a lot more besides. My father used to tell of a woman who got a very awkward choice to make. It seems that three men were put into prison for some harm that was done. They were the father, the husband, and the son of this woman. She got her choice of getting one of them out free, and the others were to go to the scaffold. She thought over it for a long time and then asked for her father to be set free. When she was asked why she selected her father she said: '*Gheobhainn fear ar tor, agus gheobhainn mac sa bhroinn, ach chá ngheobhainn athair a choíche* [I could get a man on a bush, and a son in the womb, but I could never get a father again].'

He used to tell a story of Fionn Mac Cumhaill, about one time he got lost in the forest. He sat down against the trunk of a tree to rest himself, when a *sidhe-gaoithe* [whirlwind] blew around him, and he saw a little hut among the trees straight in front of him. He got up and went inside to look for food and lodging for the night. An old grey-bearded man sat in the corner, with a big black cat on the other side of the hearth. At the other end of the hut stood a big grey ram. As Fionn entered, a very comely young girl appeared and laid a meal for him on the table. Before Fionn could get seated, the ram jumped up on the table and started to devour the food. But as he did so, the cat cut a spring and caught the ram by the throat and dragged him back to his own corner at the bottom of the hut. Fionn then got his supper in peace, and the girl showed him where he was to sleep. Fionn fell in love with the girl and begged her to come away with him and be his wife and leave that queer hut in the forest. But the girl shook her head and said: 'You had me before and you did not think much of me and threw me aside. You cannot have me again.' Fionn tried to explain that he had never set eyes on her till that day. But she only smiled and left him. Next morning Fionn found his breakfast laid on the table. Before he left he asked the old man what was the meaning of the strange household he kept. The old man said: 'I myself am Father Time and sit and watch. The ram is the World, and the black cat that keeps the world in its place is Death.'

Fionn then asked who the girl was that got him his meals. The old man replied: 'Her name is Youth. You had her once, but you can never have her again.' With that the old man rose in the air, the *sidhe-gaoithe* blew, and the hut and everything in it disappeared. Fionn found himself seated with his back against a tree in the middle of the forest.

In my early days the fair of Ballyliffin was the day for buying apples for Halloweve. We gathered nuts in the woods and saved them. Halloweve was a great time for superstitions of all kinds. Girls would be getting their fortunes told with the three plates—with clay in one, water in another, and a ring in the other. The girl would be blind-folded and whichever plate she put her hand on would mean that she would be either dead, or across water, or married before that time twelve-month. They burned nuts, too, with a boy's name on one and a girl's name on the other. If they burned together, that couple would be married. As often as not the nuts would shoot through the house.

Halloweve was a great night, too, for the fairies. They say they were able to turn benweeds into horses for themselves and would be out all night riding about on them.

I heard a story of a Magheramore man called Seán the Tailor, long ago, who was coming up Skeeog brae late one Halloweve night, when he saw a crowd of fairies riding about through a field on their horses. They called on Seán to come along with them, that they were going to Scotland. The king told him to jump on a white calf that was in the field but warned him that he was not to open his mouth or say a word till they came back home. They all set off, with Seán on the calf, till they toured Scotland and then came back across the Moyles to Malin. When they reached the Cnockamenny Bens, the horses all jumped over the bar mouth of the Isle of Doagh, the calf as well as the rest. When Seán saw the way the calf jumped, he could keep his mouth shut no longer and shouted out: 'I don't care what happens, but that

was a great jump for a calf!' With that the fairies and horses and calf
and all disappeared and Seán was left by himself down at Lagahurry in
the bottom of the isle. By the time he got back to Magheramore it was
milking-time next forenoon.

Few of the old people cared to go out late at night around
Halloweve-time.

On the Night of the Dead, the fire was never raked, but a creel of
turf was put on the fire that would last till the morning. Stools and
chairs were placed around the fire and bread and milk left on the
table. That was for people belonging to the house that were dead. It
was said they came back home for that night. Next morning, if there
was a track of a foot in the ashes, that was taken for a sign that
somebody in that house would die inside the next twelve months.

For Christmas the beef would be bought from some neighbour
man who killed a cow or a bullock. He would take the orders beforehand. A house with a big family might kill a year-old wether and salt
it and it would last till Candlemas. On Christmas Day people went in
greatly for broth thickened with oaten meal and they had beef and
soup, a thing they hadn't every day. There was always a drop of drink
going around Christmas-time and it was a great time for dancing and
big nights and gatherings of all kinds.

The Christmas rhymers always held their dances around that time.
Every band of rhymers held a dance somewhere on the money they
had collected. The dance was free for anybody who wanted to go. I
remember the rhymers' dance in the Glen in the year 1894. It was
called Donal's Ball, and nobody living that night ever forgot it. It
was the worst night's wind in living memory. The gale got up at bedtime and half the houses were stripped. (It was all thatched roofs at
that time.) When the people rushed out, the thatch and *scraths* struck
them in the face. The only safe place was under the door-head.
Gortfad was a total wreck. One blast left nothing standing but the
four walls and the couples, and the people had nothing over them but
the sky.

At the dances long ago all the mentioned singers would be there, singing the old songs, Irish ones that are forgotten now, and songs in English too. It's a pity the Irish songs were not kept up. There were no songs to equal them. The commonest songs at gatherings in my time were 'Pléaráca na bPollan' and 'Bráthair na Dumhcha'. Denis Mhichil Doherty had a song, too, that was popular. I only remember a verse of it:

Lá'l Pádraig char ghnáth liom bhéith ag cuimhead an tí,
Bhéinn in áit a mbéadh gúgán is cannaí ar an bhórd.
Is a Sheáin, a chomradaí, mura ní muid-inne póit.
Rachaidh muid amárach in áit a mbéidh an t-ól
Is muna bhfáighe muid ar cáirde é dhéanfamuidsan póit,
Is chan fhágamuid an áit seo gan cannaí móra a ól.

[*On St Patrick's Day I wouldn't be minding the house,*
I'd be off in a place where there'd be drink on the table.
And, Seán and comrades, if we don't ourselves make the drink,
We'll head tomorrow to where the drink is
And if we don't get it on credit, we'll make poteen ourselves,
And we won't depart until we have drunk a big lot.]

Denis was a great singer of the old sort.

At Christmas-time people went to visit their relations if they lived a bit away and would maybe stay the night. If it was a girl who was visiting, the people of the house got up a dance, and all the neighbours attended. There was always great run on a strange girl about a place. For the dance somebody was got to play the fiddle. Neil McColgan was the best fiddler in my time. He was a blind fiddler from Ballyliffin and was in great demand for all the dances. They made a collection at the dance of a penny a head, and that was how he made his living. He played on the boat, too, from Derry to Moville, for people who would be out pleasuring on the Foyle in the summer-time. And he used to

play on the boats going to Scotland. He got his keep on board the
boats, too, for he would draw trade to whatever boat he was on.

Neil was a noted singer and a poet too. He would not sing sitting
down. He always got to the middle of the floor and put the fiddle
under his chin and sang the song and played at the same time. One
night before Christmas in the year 1852 he was in Urris and arranged
with two lads by the name of Friel to go across with them to Fanad
next day. But Neil slept in and they went on without him. Coming
back again they brought over a young man, Hugh Friel, from Fanad,
who came over to see a girl he had married a short time before. She
was the name of McDonald, and was called the Star of Dunaff. The
boat struck a rock and the three were drowned. Neil McColgan made
a song about the drowning—'In the year of '52, in the month of
December'. I heard it sung many a time but I haven't the words of it.
The McColgans were a breed of people there was great music in.
Music is a thing that follows tribes of people.

Brigid's Eve was the night for making crosses. Before the people of
the house sat down to their supper, a girl belonging to the family went
out to bring in the rushes. If there was a girl by the name of Brigid in
the house, she got the privilege. She knocked at the door and the ones
inside said:

Oiche Bhríde brichíneach
Bain an ceann den croiceanach,
Gabhaigí ar na glúnaí,
Déanaigí umhlú
Is ligigí isteach Bríd Bheannaithe.
'Sé beatha, 'sé beatha, 'sé beatha.

[*On St Brigid's night*
Take the head off the rushes,
Go on your knees,
Make obeisance

And let St Brigid in.
You're welcome, you're welcome, you're welcome.]

That was a night my father always said the prayer 'Bail na gcúig n-arán [The blessing of the five loaves]'. After we took our supper, all the grown-up ones about the house made the rush-crosses. A cross was made for the kitchen and for above the beds and for all the outhouses.

The old people always left a rag of cloth outside on a bush that night till the morning. It had the blessing of St Brigid and was used for cures and against dangers of any kind, like the fever, or lightning, or fire, or drowning. It was called the 'Bratóg Bhríde'.

The only prayer I ever heard said after meals was '*Glór is moladh is buíochas do Dhia* [Glory and praise and thanks to God]'. Hughie Gubbin used to add another bit to it for fun '*Glór is moladh is buíochas do Dhia, is peacaí an tí seo ar an tí sin thiar* [Glory and praise and thanks to God, and may the sins of this house be on that house over there].'

All the young people in my time were getting ready for Easter long before it came. Eggs were kept for selling so we used to lift eggs and hide them so as to have a dozen or more when Easter Sunday came round. We all got together that day and made a fire outside and boiled the eggs. We ate them with flat pieces of wood that we shaped ourselves for we wouldn't get spoons out with us.

Before this nobody would go to bathe in the salt water till after Whit Sunday. People had a notion that it was dangerous. I always heard, too, that it wasn't a lucky day to be born, that a human being or an animal born on that day would do some harm or get a violent death. A foal born on that day was considered a dangerous animal.

The bonfire night was a great gathering night for young and old. It comes at a time of year when people can be out, and sure you may say there's no night in it at mid-summer. Every townland gathered sticks and bushes and turf for the bonfire. It was the custom long ago to drive cattle through the ashes of the bonfire and then to take the burnt sticks and throw some into the crops and the outhouses. Nearly all these customs are done away with now. The bonfires are lit in lots of places yet but they are nothing like what they used to be.

Heather-berry Sunday, too, was a great day in this parish. It fell on the last Sunday in July. The young people all went to the hills on that day, gathering bilberries and heather-berries. It was a big day when I was growing up but there are people going now who never heard of it.

Chapter Eighteen

Epilogue

WHEN I WAS ABOUT SIXTEEN YEARS of age I started learning the weaving trade from my father. I knew a lot about it beforehand, looking at him and trying my hand now and again. I liked the work of weaving, and it was a thing came naturally to my hand. I spent many a night at the loom, weaving, when other young fellows of my age were away ceilidhing or *regaiding* [gossiping] or dancing. I made many a half-crown that way in the winter nights.

I was a good hand at creels and baskets, too, and I often made them by the firelight at night by taking in a sod to stick the uprights in. I made a kind of a currach one time with rods and covered it with paper and tar and bags, but it was swept down the river one night by a big flood, and I never got hilt or hair of it after.

As I grew up, the home weaving was falling away and there wasn't a great living in it later on. Times were changing. When I was drawing up on thirty, the weaving was slack and I went over to the harvest one year with others from these parts. I carried a bundle with a change of shirts and socks and went in my working clothes. I took the boat from Derry to Glasgow and then the train to Berwick-on-Tweed where I was to get work on a farm. The work was shearing and lifting corn and the wages were £1 a week with my keep. I was given a blanket and slept on straw in the barn.

I only went over the one year. I had enough to do at home for I was the only boy of the family left at home.

Fanny, the oldest of the family, went to America about the time I was born. She got married to a man named Kinsella and they lived in

Stockbridge some way out of Boston and had a family. Her husband got blown up in a quarry and was killed.

About that time an older brother, Owen, went to America, too, and spent nearly all his life in the navy there and travelled to all parts of the world. He never got married. The next after Owen died at home with the fever. The fever took away a lot of people before this.

My youngest brother, Neil, went to the harvest in Scotland one year and one warm day he went into some river or place for bathing and was drowned. The place was called Broxburn. He was buried there.

I had another brother, Patrick, who was two years younger than I was. He got more schooling than I did. The younger ones generally got a better chance. He was clever and could read English well and Irish, too, and didn't leave school till he was as far on as the master could put him. After he left school he was fond of reading books and papers, and carried a book with him when he went out to herd the cows. He got some books about the shorthand writing and picked up the shorthand himself out of the books and could write it well. On Sundays, when the parish priest was preaching, Patrick wrote down what he said in shorthand and could give out the whole sermon again when he came home. The people at that time thought it was one of the greatest wonders of the world and nothing short of a miracle, how anybody could do it.

When he was nineteen, he made up his mind to enter the Trappist monastery in Waterford and wrote to the Lord Abbot in Mount Melleray. He got back a form and filled it in. Fr Doherty, the parish priest, must have got a letter from the Lord Abbot about him, for one Sunday not long after he spoke to my father about it and asked if he was willing to let him go. My father said he would let him please himself.

He went away in 1883. Brother Bernard was the name he took in religion. He wrote letters home but did not give much news about himself, but in one of them he mentioned that his health was not too good. Then in 1897 I got a letter from one of the brothers to say that

Patrick had died some days before that. He lived only fourteen years in the monastery.

My father had died some years before that, and then in 1914 my mother died, and a couple of years later my sister, Síle. She never got married.

I am the only one of the name that is left now. I never got married myself for I never had a rid house or a way of marrying till it was past my time. I got a long life and have a lot to be thankful for. I often noticed, when one member of a family is left after the others die early or in middle age, that that person generally takes a long life.

In my time I have seen six or seven generations of people, and lots of things I see happening today are not to be wondered at, for there are things that run in breeds of people and come out somewhere in nearly every generation. A weakness for drink follows certain families, and stealing and dishonesty can be traced in breeds of people as far back as memory goes. The old people called that a *dúchas*. But the old people always said that drink was a thing no man had to hang his head for. Insanity, too, follows people, but it is not as common as it was, for in times ago there were more sib marriages than now. Men wouldn't leave their own townland when looking for a wife, till they would be all related through other. By-children [illegitimate children], too, follow certain breeds, and there are some that leave nothing at all behind.

But it ill becomes any of us to be too uncharitable. There was an old saying common long ago that would apply to most people: 'Sa choill is feárr, gheobhaidh tú oiread brosna is a dhoghfas chun talaimh i [In the cleanest forest that ever grew, you will find as much twigs as will burn it to the ground].'

With all the changes I have seen in the world in my time, I have come to the stage where I would be surprised at nothing. I often wondered what Eibhlin Roddy or the Daisy—that was her mother— would think if they could come back for a Sunday afternoon along the Glen road and see the buses and cars and the silk stockings and the style that's going now. I think a while of an hour would do them. They would wonder what the world was coming to.

I had a long life and I must be thankful for I always had the best of health. I never had an hour's sickness in my life and I don't know what toothache is. I was ninety-two last Christmas and I have every tooth in my head yet. There is no doctor ever got a penny of my money. I was attended by the priest once, but that was one evening a few years ago that I took a weak turn on the roadside, and the neighbours got the priest without getting my permission. I apologised for putting the journey on him and explained how it happened. I told him, when I was able to do without sending for a priest for over four score years, that it was hardly worth my while starting. He was a Dr Collins who was afterwards made parish priest of Gortin. I said the *Confiteor* for him in Latin and in Irish, to let him see I wasn't as far through as the people made out. I learned the Latin from listening to the clerks at Mass on a Sunday.

But my time on this world must be getting short. The people I knew and grew up along with are nearly all gone before me. Over our grave there was always an old quarry flag, but it was getting sunk in the ground with grass growing over it. So ten or twelve years ago I gave an order for a new one to Owen Roddy. The making of it cost £5, but I was out the best part of £6 to get it erected, with the price of drink and all. A pound doesn't go far on drink these times.

So, whenever I die, they will know where to bury me. And after my day the grave will not be opened again, for I'm the last of the name. And when I do go and fall in with Paddy Mór Roddy and the Ogaster and Eibhlin and Eoin O Kerrigan and all the rest, sure I'll be no stranger to them.